MAKING SPIRIT-LED DECISIONS

A GUIDE TO CONFIDENT ANSWERS FOR YOUR RELATIONSHIP DOUBTS

GINNY ELLSWORTH

CONTENTS

Pure Southern Ink, LLC

Nashville, TN, USA

Original publication 2020

Second edition published 2023

ISBN 978-1-7341436-6-9 (paperback)

ISBN 978-1-7341436-7-6 (eBook)

ISBN 978-1-7341436-9-0 (audiobook)

DISCLAIMER

Neither the author nor the publisher assumes any responsibility for errors, omissions, or contrary interpretations of the subject matter herein. Any perceived slight of any individual or organization is purely unintentional.

This publication is designed to provide accurate and authoritative information in regard to the subject matter covered. It is sold with the understanding that neither the author nor the publisher is engaged in rendering legal, investment, accounting, or medical services. While the publisher and author have used their best efforts in preparing this book, they make no representations or warranties with respect to the accuracy or completeness of the contents of this book and specifically disclaim any implied warranties of merchantability or fitness for a particular purpose. No warranty may be created or extended by sales representatives or written sales materials. The advice and strategies contained herein may not be suitable for

FOREWORD BY SUE BUCHANAN
AUTHOR, SPEAKER, LITERARY CONSULTANT

To Ginny's readers:

There is a mandate that was ingrained into my psyche for as long as I can remember. *Pray and read the Bible.* I've done a lot of that in my time, although not as much as you'd think, given my short attention span, my dyslexia, and probably, though undiagnosed, ADHD. Or is it DHDA?

In my day (don't ask!) you didn't question adults, much less the people in my *don't dance, don't chew, and don't go out with boys who do,* fundamentalists church. Make no mistake, I will be eternally grateful for those God-fearing souls who taught me to love scripture, and to make it part of my everyday living. But those rules! Those BRULES! The meaning of which you will learn in this book! (No jumping ahead!)

One thing we didn't talk about in my church is the Holy Spirit! In fact, we were warned about "those Pentecostals who spoke in tongues and rolled in the aisles." Truth be told, I probably would have dabbled in serpent handling given my obsessive curiosity, which I possess to this day.

I'm writing this foreword to Ginny's book to tell you: "Don't miss this one factor that would have changed my whole life, and the lives of my children, and the audience that has read my books and come to hear me speak." While Ginny speaks specifically to making decisions about relationships, it applies to life in the broadest sense.

I've watched the stages of Ginny's life—she has called me Aunt Sue for most of that life—and I have to admit to thinking "poor girl, she's never gonna get through this"—whatever the *this* was at the moment. But get through she did! Sometimes hanging on by bloody—though well-manicured —fingertips.

In this book she nakedly pours out the mistakes and the wrong thinking she had to slog through to get to where she is now.

Her book is born of question marks. "Is it a mistake to marry this man?" "What should I do next?" "How should I react?" "How did I get myself into this fix?" "Which voices should I listen to?" "Why am I so wishy-washy in my decision making?" "Why in the world did I do THAT?"

The answer Ginny discovers, is within that darling package that is her body, is driven by that crazy curious mind, and is honed deep within that heart of hers—a heart that pounds with love and cartwheels of joy for God.

Whatever you call it—that still small voice, that true north, your internal compass, your intuition, your conscience . . . or passing the sniff test. Ginny has found it. And why not? She keeps reminding us that we are fearfully and wonderfully made and with that in mind, it's only reasonable to believe we came equipped with tools for life-building.

I can't wait to use this book in counseling, where the first question I hear is, "I don't know if I'm making a mistake. How am I supposed to know?" I can't wait to encourage others to (after honest prayer) trust that still small voice . . . that *knowing*.

Scripture tells us the Holy Spirit is given to us for our comfort, and to my way of thinking, comfort comes in *the knowing*. Ginny Ellsworth has taken me to this sacred place of knowing, and she can take you there as well.

" All changes in the quality of life must grow out of a change in our vision of reality.

— BRENNAN MANNING, AUTHOR, SPEAKER, ONE-TIME FRANCISCAN PRIEST, AND UNCONVENTIONAL EVANGELIST

To help you navigate the content in this book and get the most out of the process we walk through, I've put together some resources. Scan the QR code to download worksheets and meditations to accompany this book.

The beauty of making spirit-led decisions is it's a skill you can continue to refine as you lean into the work. There will be seasons of life when decisions feel tough and sticky and confusing, and seasons where your answers feel effortlessly crystal clear. My wish for you is that you always have a process you're comfortable coming back to no matter the situation. You are not alone.

XO,
Ginny

You fell in love with the man of your dreams. The vision of your picture-perfect life together naturally evolved, like magic that was meant to be. Yet, down the road, you found yourself stuck in a life you didn't sign up for. This is not what you planned. You convinced everyone (including yourself) that this guy was the one, that he was perfect for you. Maybe you walked down the aisle. Maybe you build a decades-long marriage. What will other people think if you end this relationship? Is it worth the embarrassment? Will staying turn you into someone you don't want to be? (Has it already?)

Life-altering decisions can be paralyzing. Perfectionism and fear of failure and disappointment can stop us in our tracks.

If you're finding yourself at a place in life you never thought you'd be, and you don't know which way to go, give yourself some grace. No matter what outside influences might say, it's not as easy as just choosing. You might love your partner—but you know things can't keep going on like they have been. Maybe he is not a bad guy; things just aren't working out. Maybe he *is* a bad guy, but you've got to do what you think is best for the kids, and maybe, for you, that includes having parents who are together. Every day, this decision hovers over you, staring you down like an endless game of don't-blink. And every day that you wrestle with the decision to stay in this relationship or go, you lose a piece of yourself. The dreams you had for your life slip further and further away.

But this decision is not just about you. It's going to affect everyone around you. It will affect the kids. It will affect your friends . . . *Wait!* The friends. Who will get the friends? Will they take sides? Will they try to remain neutral? Maybe some of them see it coming. Maybe they are already making guesses about whether you two will make it.

It gets worse. Outside of you, your partner, the kids, and your closest circle of friends, you find the most complex part of the whole decision: your parents, his parents, and the church. If church isn't your thing, think of your spiritual community, or the community you turn to for standards. There could be more than one group that represents this area in your life. How will you explain ending this relationship? How will you explain staying? What will they think? Should you let them weigh in on this decision?

I've been there too. For most of my life, in every decision (except maybe what's for dinner), letting everyone else weigh in has been my go-to. I tend to run every big situation by my most trusted circle. In major decisions, my circle's opinion matters the most to me. I convince myself that they will know what I should do, better than I do. In fact, their opinion matters more to me than my own does. There've been decision-making times in my life where I crowdsourced so many opinions that I didn't even know what my own opinion was. The abundance of "good points" and everyone else's pros and cons created a haze that blocked my own feelings and inner wisdom.

Here's the thing. (Yikes, I just said "Here's the thing," the phrase an old friend uses before he dishes out some cold hard truth.) Okay, so here's the thing: This decision is way more complex than just choosing to leave your relationship or not. What led you to this place was a series of decisions, each of which you most likely made the same way you've always made your decisions: by considering everyone else first.

I'm not going to tell you to be selfish. I'm not going to tell you to run for the hills or to get divorced. That is not what this book is about. This book is about making Spirit-led decisions. It's about quieting the outside noise so you can hear your own voice—the voice that has probably been muffled for longer than you care to remember—and hear divine guidance.

God gives us the desires of our hearts. Of course, there are several ways to interpret that, but initially, I would like to think that God places desires in our hearts. You have an inner voice. Sure, that voice is partially you (And guess what? It's okay to listen to *you* and choose for *you*.), but that inner voice is also from Spirit, from the source, from your true north.

Throughout this book I'm going to use God, the Universe, Spirit, intuition, inner voice, and maybe some other terms. These terms are not limited to a religion or a certain way of thinking. They are universal, and I hope that within the context you'll feel there meaning. If something doesn't sit well with you, use a term that does. It's the heart of the term that matters.

Having grown up very involved in church, I agree that the Spirit can speak through other people, but if you already struggle with people-pleasing or perfectionism (or both, like I do), it's going to be really hard to distinguish the voice of the Spirit from the voice of your friends (or family members) seeping in. The problem with searching for an answer outside of yourself is that, naturally, you care what all of those outside sources think because you love them.

The safest place to find the voice of the Spirit is inside *you*.

I know that is *way* easier said than done. I know because I have been there too, *so* many times. I'm a pro at justifying things, so much so that my mother used to say I had the gift of persuasion. Let me tell you from experience, being great at arguing both sides is a great way to stay stuck in indecision. How do you get out of that sticky no-man's-land? The best thing to do is to step outside of everyone else's thoughts and opinions.

Let's go back to the series of decisions that brought you here. Maybe you committed to this guy because you fell in love with him. Maybe you committed to this guy because *everyone else* fell in love with him. Maybe he is not living up to your expectations—or maybe he is not living up to *everyone else's* expectations for you or for your relationship.

Do you see how complicated this gets? This is not a one-time, targeted, life-altering decision. Where you are now is the result of layers of decisions.

If your palms are sweaty and your heart is racing because you're now feeling even more pressure, take a deep breath, and do not worry. I am not only going to help guide you through this huge decision, but I'm also going to equip you with tools you can use to make future decisions, big or small. Growing up, I was taught that God is with us. He doesn't leave us or forsake us (Deuteronomy 31:6). To this day, I truly believe that, even after all that I've been through. He is with us in the mess, even if we created the mess. God is the redeemer of the mess.

Can we take a little break from the seriousness for a minute? Thinking about the mess, I'm reminded of one of my mom's favorite stories from when I was in Sunday school. In our two-year-old class at church, we were learning about how God made everything. Well, that message stuck with me. One afternoon during the week, I was sent to my room for quiet time (aka Mom's break—ya hear me, moms?). When my mom came back to check on me,

I had pulled every book off my shelf and every toy out of its place and had piled everything in the middle of my floor (because what two-year-old girl doesn't want to sit in the middle of all her stuff? *insert queen emoji*).

Mom opened the door and gasped. "Ginny! Who made this mess?" she exclaimed, slightly horrified that her break time had resulted in probably an hour's worth of helping me pick up.

"God did!" I looked up and smiled, knowing I had the right answer.

That moment is not unlike my life! Sometimes I feel like I'm just sitting in the middle of my giant mess—a mess that I made, a mess that is the result of what I feel are "bad" decisions. But God is there. He is there in the mess with you, and guess what: he is not judging you. *Whoa.* No judgment? What does that even feel like? We are so good at making judgments and labeling things as black or white, but life isn't always black and white. Sometimes it's gray. Sometimes it's so gray you can't see what is in front of you. There is a way through that gray fog, a way to see God in the mess, and a way to see *his* way of bringing order back to it.

I've always envied my friends who don't care what everyone else thinks, because, well, I have always cared what other people think. Some of that was definitely a learned behavior, fostered by a strict environment, but some of it, I have to believe, is just nature. I love people. I love the people around me, and I want them to love me back. I want to make my family proud. I want to be a strong person who achieves a lot in this life and is recognized for it. Well, I used to, anyway. Breaking the mindset of perfectionism and people-pleasing is a process. It's not something you just wake up and stop doing one day. You don't just stop caring. It very well might be your nature to care.

So, let's look at perfectionism and people-pleasing in light of where you are in life right now. Although they are not the same thing, they are closely related. Perfectionism is wanting to get whatever it is that you are doing exactly right. People-pleasing is wanting to make everyone else happy.

Let me ask you this, dear Perfectionist: Why do you want to get everything exactly right? To make everyone else happy? *Ohhh.* You see where I'm going with this?

The problem with trying to step outside of the old habits of perfectionism and people-pleasing in order to make a big decision is that other influences still sneak in.

Let me give you an example. When conversations about marriage started infiltrating a relationship in

my early thirties, naturally, I crowdsourced my opinion. I talked to my best friend. I talked to my
parents. They all had valid sentiments: "He seems
like a great guy. Sure, he has kids," which was not
something I was looking for, "but at this point in
your life, a lot of great guys are going to have kids."
They made a good point. "Being in a serious relationship will create stability and get you to settle down."
That felt true, since I was traveling for work literally
all the time. I was rarely home, and the only things
that felt stable were my Monday morning flight and
whirlwind weekends of trying to maintain some
semblance of a social life, spend time with my family,
and do the unpack–wash laundry–repack routine. So,
it sure sounded like choosing marriage was choosing
for me.

Nope. I was still listening to what everyone else
thought was best for me. I still compromised what I
actually wanted and explained it away with "But so-
and-so said . . . and that made sense." If I didn't
settle down and get married, would they think I was
a lost cause? Would they think I didn't want those
things one day? Would they think my career was
more important to me than family and building a life
at home? Thoughts like these are sneaky, especially
when they've been with you for nearly your entire
life!

Fear of failure goes hand in hand with perfectionism and people-pleasing. No one *likes* to fail, but for some of us, failure feels like the end of the world. And in the midst of choosing whether you should fight for your relationship or call it quits, you probably feel like you have failed at *something*. You might feel like your relationship is already a failure or like you failed in that initial decision to commit and now you have to redeem it.

Maybe you have tried everything you can. If you could just get your partner to change, maybe you could save your relationship. If you could just find the right counselor to help him see the problem, things would be different. Umm, remember the mess? *You* are not the redeemer. Our brains naturally want to make sense of it all, but it's not up to you to find a way to cover your bad-decision tracks. It's time to stop the what-ifs, look at what is really there, and make decisions based on reality. We are going to do that together.

However failure has shown up in this relationship—maybe in your initial decision to commit to this guy or maybe in the situation not meeting your expectations—you might now find yourself frantically trying to cover up that failure. Maybe you're even covering it up in front of him. Maybe you're sacrificing pieces of who you are to try to make it work. Maybe you're covering it up in front of your friends or your parents, trying to hide the relationship flaws and give the perception that everything is going as planned. But the person you have no doubt disappointed the most is yourself.

You're disappointed in yourself because you've failed everyone else. They believed you when you convinced them that he was the one. They believed you when you painted the mental picture of what your life would be like. Shoot, *you* believed you too! So now—to compound an already complex decision —you don't trust yourself, which, might I add, makes it all the easier to let in those outside voices. You *trust* those people. They are your friends, your family, the people who really care about you. But there is a vicious cycle. You don't trust yourself, so you base your decisions on other people's input (even if you don't realize it). This perpetuates the pressure to choose what they want for you—and when you do that, you've now added the pressure of getting it right, making it right even if it's not, and keeping it right. And if you don't? Well, failure . . . losing trust in yourself . . . and the cycle begins again.

Ouch. Thinking about it will make you crazy. I'm here to tell you that I've been there, and there is a way out. There is a way out of this stuckness, and whether you choose to stay in this relationship or to go, choose for you—the real you. Listen to that whisper—the one inside you—and let that be the only thing that influences you.

I can't change your past. *You* can't change your past. But you can build your beautiful, bright, Spirit-led future. You have the power to create a life that you are proud of. You have the power to own your story and let God use it in a way you'd never imagine.

Where you are right now is not an accident. No matter what your thoughts might be telling you, your current circumstances are not the result of a string of failures. They are your story. You may not know why this is your story, but it's your story for a reason—and when you own it, when you let the power within you come forward, that is when the Spirit redeems your beautiful mess.

   *As for me, I know that my Redeemer lives.*

— JOB 19:25 (NLT)

2

A RUINED LIFE

REDEEMED

There I was, alone in an empty apartment 809 miles away from home. I had nothing. Later, I would meet up with a friend to borrow her inflatable mattress, a couple of pillows, and a set of sheets. But for the moment, I was lying on the floor in a slobbery puddle of tears. How had I gotten here? How was I supposed to face this?

I was lucky; despite the best efforts of my (almost ex-) husband, after agreeing to move to Texas to be with him and to take a position at a new magazine, I had gotten involved with a local nonprofit. Don't get me wrong, he had made me pay for it. He hadn't wanted me to do anything outside of working and taking care of his kids. In fact, after only six months, I'd left the killer job I'd landed before my official move and taken a 50 percent pay cut because he had wanted me home earlier in the evening without the long commute. I had sobbed my way through that decision too, but I hadn't known what else to do. I had made a commitment to this marriage.

Anyway, back to the nonprofit. It was another one of those things he hadn't wanted me involved in. It was all women, so he couldn't participate outside of family events, but I had approached my involvement like it wasn't an option: "I'm going to join the Service League. It's the best way for me to get involved in the community and make friends here." Service League supported multiple nonprofits in the county, and each member chose one of those nonprofits to focus on for the year. He reluctantly agreed under the condition that I focus on the nonprofit that was most connected to his job at child protective services. So, I had agreed. He and I had both known that was his effort to keep an eye on me, keeping an element of control.

Nevertheless, it was the involvement with that group of women that was saving me now. Even though hadn't allowed me to participate in anything outside of the minimum requirements, I, of course, still managed to make friends—and these girlfriends were now rallying around me at literally the worst time in my life.

Some of you might recognize this scenario as abuse, and you are correct. This was one of endless examples of abuse in that relationship. If you don't recognize that situation as abuse but can relate to it, I strongly recommend you jot down the similarities and other situations that bring up the same emotions. This book is not about abusive relationships; it's about making a decision to stay or to go, whether or not abuse is involved. However, if you do find yourself in an abusive relationship or have questions about what that looks like, I've included some good resources in chapter 13 to help you.

That day on the floor, I questioned everything—and I mean *everything*. All of the decisions I had made that led me to this place, this soggy spot on the floor of an empty third-floor apartment. If I had not chosen to stay in town over a long weekend when I was working in Texas, I never would have met him. When he sat down at the table next to me and told me basically his life story, I had heard a whisper inside that said, "This guy is a train wreck. Get up and go find your friends." I chose to ignore it. And now, taking a 50 percent pay cut, staying after his violent outbursts . . . How had I gotten here? I had thought I was doing the right thing—every step of the way, I had thought I was doing the right thing. Other than ignoring that initial voice, where had I gone wrong?

Although our marriage had happened quickly (which I found out later was his mode of operation), I had talked to my parents about it; they seemed to love him. My best friend had approved, even after going over all my reservations. And therein lies the problem: I had let everyone else make the decision for me. Instead of digging down deep to find out what I wanted, I had let everyone else's opinions override my inner voice—only to find myself in a relationship where I wasn't allowed to make my own decisions.

Don't get me wrong, there was a big part of me that had wanted to marry him, but I had wanted to marry the person I had thought he was. I had ignored all the red flags in an effort to capture the dream. I remember sitting outside Starbucks with my friend Jocelyn. Jocelyn and I had sparked a friendship more than a decade before in Austin while working for 24 Hour Fitness, and we had gotten back in touch when I'd moved to Houston and realized she was living there too. Although we weren't (and still aren't) the best at keeping in touch, we have one of those friendships that picks up right where we left off. We can tell each other anything without judgment, and she always brings an objective view and voice of reason to any situation.

"I think I should get an annulment. I don't know what to do, Jocelyn," I confessed on the Starbucks patio, Joel Osteen's megachurch in the background.

Jocelyn affectionately referred to that location as Joel's Starbucks. She was the only person who knew that we had gotten married two months before our actual wedding. He had insisted on it so that we could buy a house. We needed both his VA loan qualification and my income (and down payment— ugh, thinking about that still makes me sick).

The night before I met up with Jocelyn, my new secret husband had had one of his violent outbursts and had tried to throw me out of the apartment, saying that I wasn't on the lease and that he was going to call the police because he didn't want me there anymore. (I guess he had forgotten we had gotten married the week before.) A conversation about how he wanted me to quit my (new) job had set him off, and I had brushed it off as stress of a new living situation, our upcoming wedding, the kids adjusting, really any excuse I could find—not because I necessarily wanted to stay, but more because I didn't know where else to go. I still had two weeks to file an annulment, but I would need a plan, a place to live, and a way to safely get my things, including my dog, out of his apartment.

"Whatever you decide, GinGin." Jocelyn still called me by the nickname that only my family used and that she had adopted when we had met more than a decade before. "I'll support you."

A year and a half after our courthouse marriage, a year and a half of surviving and fighting, it was over. I had prayed my way through most of it. My very last prayer in that relationship was "God, if you want me out of this, you're going to have to give me no option to stay. I can't walk away on my own," and he gave me what I'd asked for—although a slightly softer letdown would have been nice. I was violently thrown out of my own house (yes, the house with my down payment and my name on it) with the threat of "you're not safe here anymore," a statement he followed me around whispering in a creepy voice while I baked a birthday cake for his son, eventually shouting it when the kids were out of sight.

I remember talking to one of the officers who responded to my 911 call later that night. As I threw some clothes in a bag, he said, "If your name is on the house, you don't have to leave, but I can't do anything about him if he didn't directly say he was going to kill you." (Looking back, I recognize that he was trying to help by hinting at what I should tell him.)

"I won't be alive in the morning if I stay," I responded, my brain swimming in confusion and terror.

I had survived an abusive relationship. That divorce was extremely justified, so why the immense amount of shame and slew of life questions that day in the empty apartment? I've always been the type to brush my knees off and keep going, so why the puddle on the floor? Well, that wasn't my first divorce—at the ripe old age of thirty-two, it was my second. Cue the crowd of shaming voices.

I grew up in the church. In fact, my parents were founding members of the church we attended throughout my childhood. My mother was pregnant with me when the group met for their first service in the gymnasium of Hillsboro High School in Nashville. The church grew, and I grew along with it. Property was purchased, a building built, and an academy launched as a ministry of the church. I was on church property at least six days out of every week. The daughter of a Southern Baptist minister, my mother had grown up in a family where, if the church doors were open, you were there, and that is how my brother and I were raised.

During the school year, we attended the academy. When I was old enough, I volunteered in the children's ministry, helped run Vacation Bible Schools in the summer, mentored younger girls, and was on the youth group worship team. I played by the rules, and even though the academy had become a competitive prep school by the time I hit high school, I had still managed to keep my faith at the forefront.

In fact, after my freshman year, I'd taken the summer to participate in a two-month-long mission trip. Kids from all over the country gathered and were divided into groups and sent off to visit different churches and communities all over the globe. It was a blast; it was the first thing I'd done that wasn't directly connected to the church I grew up in, and the following summer, I did it again. That is where I met my first husband.

Now that guy, I didn't really want to marry, but it just seemed like what I was supposed to do. Although he was seven years my senior (which when you're still in high school is a huge difference), my mother loved him. Even though our relationship was long distance, he had been supportive of my decision to go to college a year early (I was feeling squashed in that competitive prep school after spending summers in underdeveloped countries across the globe). He checked all the boxes on paper, and according to the rule book, that's who I was supposed to marry.

Somehow, we both landed in Southern California —I was attending Azusa Pacific, a private, missions-focused, Christian university, and he had been stationed at Camp Pendleton. He was deployed for most of our marriage, and when he was home, I found myself on antidepressants. His controlling nature was stealthy. He truly thought he was doing the right thing by controlling his family (me).

I will spare you further details. To be honest, many of them have been pushed to a hidden part of my brain that I choose not to revisit.

I remember the day of our wedding. I was in the bridal suite, having been the first one to arrive at the church; my mom was buzzing around somewhere, making sure everything was just perfect, I'm sure. I stared into the mirror, and my thought, to this day, is a vivid memory: "I don't want to do this, but I don't know how to get out of it."

My bridesmaids were on their way. More than 300 friends and family members would be gathering soon. My mother and I had meticulously put together every detail, careful not to leave anyone out and conscious of keeping everyone happy. Even people who fell into the category of "you don't know her but she prays for you" were invited. My fiancé's sister would be singing, since I already had too many bridesmaids but she "needed" to be in the wedding. His father would be officiating. My oldest cousin was a bridesmaid because my mom, my aunt, and my grandmother insisted that I have a family member in my court since I didn't have a sister. It was everyone's day, and I didn't mind because it was everyone I loved. In the end, we had a blast. We danced the night away.

But at twenty years old, I had stared in that mirror, knowing I didn't want this. Knowing I was much too independent to marry such a controlling man. Knowing there was no spark. But feeling like I had to do it anyway. I had to do it for everyone else.

And no, we had not had sex, so Purity Culture-induced guilt from that was not a factor. Which brings me back to my point: I had followed all the rules. So how did I end up, years later, twice divorced, with not even a pillowcase to my name?

In my first marriage, I had stayed much longer than I should have, simply because I was too young and naive and didn't know that there was such a thing as emotional and verbal abuse. But the first shove across the room I got gave me permission to go. Again, I remember very little about that time in my life (I know, I probably need to let it surface and work through the scars), but I do remember sneaking away to counseling every week. I remember being nervous. I remember learning to identify the degrading thoughts that were planted in my head and to "change the story"—and I remember feeling like a lost puppy when I finally left.

I did what I needed to do to protect myself, but what now? Where would I go? What was I supposed to do with my life? I had quit my job to move back home and get my feet on the ground. I taught preschool at my childhood church two days a week, I waited tables six days a week, and I started building up personal training clients in Tennessee. I did what I needed to do to keep moving forward, even though I had no idea where I was going. It was like someone had thrown water all over my life instructions—the clear words had been smeared beyond recognition.

So why on Earth would you listen to me, a twice-divorced ginormous failure? Well, because I'm a twice-divorced "ginormous failure" who has let God transform my story into something more magnificent than I would have ever written for myself. I remember one thought I had had that day on the floor of my empty apartment, soaked in tears, just as vividly as the thought I had had before my first wedding. Through sips of air and probably a snort, I had sat up and thought, *I don't know why this is my story, but it is* my *story. It is my story for a reason, even if I can't see the reason right now, and I am going to own it.*

Thinking of all of the embarrassment that I was about to face—the shame of not one scarlet letter but two—I knew I could face it, if God could use it. After all, my Redeemer lives.

Fast-forward several years later, still in Texas, I had moved "into town." I mean, y'all, you can drive for two hours straight and still be in Houston—four hours if there's traffic! It took me two years after that divorce to rally the courage to leave my girl-friends in the 'burbs and move to an area closer to my new job—and let's be honest, with a better singles' scene. The church I'd been attending in the suburbs was planting a church in town, and I decided that would be my first go-to to build community—although I did give myself permission to check out other churches if I didn't feel connected.

But I did. The first Sunday that I went, I was met at the door by the campus pastor (whose wife is now a dear friend of mine) and then was introduced to the women's pastor, who immediately connected me with women who—although they are now scattered across the state (and the globe)—are still supportive friends to this day. The church was small, meeting in a gymnasium of a local high school, and of course I began volunteering in the children's ministry.

About a year later, we had moved into a building and were ready to officially launch in the community. The majority of ladies in our small women's group were "voluntold" that we would each be leading a table during the weekly women's Bible study. Part of our assignment at the first gathering was to share our stories, within the context of two "bad" things that had happened to us and two "good" things, and to explain how each of the four events changed us. At this point in my life, there was no shortage of "bad" things to choose from: two divorces, my mom's death, my condo flooding (only once at that point), but after a week of prayer, I felt strongly that I was supposed to share each divorce on its own, each as an individual "bad" thing.

This was *terrifying*. I rarely mentioned divorce at all, even outside of church. In fact, I never even thought about my first marriage, and my second was quickly fading into something that felt like a bad dream. "I'm supposed to be leading these women in *Bible study*," I remember arguing out loud with God. "I can't tell them I've been divorced not once but *twice*." But he wouldn't take no for an answer, so— before I got caught in whatever the modern-day version of the belly of the whale is—I agreed and did it.

You see, years before, I had "owned" my story. Well, I had owned it to the people who already knew it, but sharing it, especially at church, was something I dodged like a champ. I knew it was a powerful one, I knew God was doing something powerful through it, but I still carried a tremendous amount of shame around with it. I guess hadn't really owned it—more like I had claimed it, but I hadn't learned to love it. In fact, I hadn't even learned to be okay with it.

I was among the first group of thirteen people to be baptized at that church. It was a special group, and although I'd had the opportunity to be baptized before, I had never felt a strong pull to take part—at least, not the kind of pull I felt this time. I didn't really know what to make of it—what transformation was I looking for? I'd been sprinkled as an infant. (My mom grew up Southern Baptist and my dad grew up Catholic. So, they compromised and raised my brother and me in the Presbyterian church. And Presbyterians don't dunk, they sprinkle—and they'll say it to ya, just like that.) I remember my prayer before that dunking baptism: "God, I want things to be different. No turning back—different." I wasn't asking for a new husband; I wasn't asking for a new house; I didn't need a new life; I just wanted different, even though I couldn't identify what that looked like.

And different it was. Looking back, I can see how both of those events, sharing my story and getting baptized, were a turning point in my spiritual journey and my personal growth. Being open about my past was liberating. I saw that people still loved me for who I was. I saw that "twice divorced" was not my identity. It didn't define me, and it no longer had power over me. People began to enter my life, even outside of the church, people who challenged me and fostered my transformation. I've grown more spiritually in the last several years than I have maybe ever, and certainly mountains more than when I was letting my past—my story—hold me back.

Through this growth, I've been able to look back at my major decisions—including both marriages, both divorces, going to college early, the decision to buy a home that, as it turns out, floods every time it rains (welcome to Houston)—and I've been able to identify my motivations behind those decisions. I now have the skills to identify all the outside voices (you know, all those people you want to make happy, all those people you can't say no to), quiet their influence, and go within to listen to my inner guidance. Sure, if I had known then what I know now, I would've made different decisions, but then my story would be different, and I wouldn't be here helping you rewrite yours.

> *In all this you greatly rejoice, though now for a little while you may have had to suffer grief in all kinds of trials. These have come so that the proven genuineness of your faith.*
>
> — 1 PETER 1:6 (NIV)

3
THE HEART'S
TUG-OF-WAR

Staying in, fighting for, or leaving your relationship might be the hardest decision you've ever had to face. Rather than telling you what to do, I'm going to guide you through the process of calling out your people-pleaser, dropping expectations, and quieting outside voices so you can hear your inner voice, your intuition, and the answer that you'll never doubt.

Being part of a failing relationship, or even one that is just starting to show cracks, can feel like a trap. You start reacting in an effort to keep the status quo or to grasp for what you previously had. That's the scary thing about reactions—they easily spin a web that is hard to find your way out of. And before you know it, you've lost your way, and even yourself. The good news is you already have everything you need to get back on track—to escape the sticky mess. You just have to be able to hear it, feel it, see it. I'm going to show you how.

When you're done reading this book, you're going to be able to identify when you're blaming someone else and take responsibility for moving forward without shame. Stopping blame in its tracks will slow down that reactive state and help bring you back to stability. (Whether you realize it or not, just the emotional state and mindset of stability will help you physically feel better and also help you make clearer decisions.) You might not even be blaming someone else; you might be blaming yourself and reacting from there. Either way, blame sends you on a downward spiral that feels impossible to get out of. When you're able to call out blame and see the situation for what it really is, you'll be able to take clear action that you feel confident about.

Blame is heavily linked to expectations, which we are going to dissect in chapter 4. When we expect a specific outcome from someone (including ourselves) and we don't get it, in comes blame. Naturally, blame is the easiest way to deal with the disappointment of the unmet expectations. But let me tell you something about blame: it will keep you stuck. There is a huge difference between fault and responsibility. Just because someone is at fault does not mean it is their responsibility to repair the situa-tion. Sure, that would be nice in a perfect world, but don't hold your breath.

Have you ever met someone who continues to blame their parents for their life or the way they turned out? It's exhausting. I've come across people whose idea of healing their life was telling their parents what an awful childhood they had. It made me want to scream. Sure, bad things happen to everyone, and many of them are someone else's fault, but whose responsibility is it to move forward? *Yours.* You cannot control other people's choices. You can't change your past. But you can choose to move forward—and moving forward feels so good!

We're going to poke gigantic holes in your fear of failure and your people-pleasing habits by leveling the playing field with a proven method. We are going to spend an entire chapter on expectations—and not just the expectations that you have of others, but the expectations that others have of you, the expecta-tions you have of yourself, and how all of these versions of expectations affect your relationship, whether you realize it or not. That leads us into comparisons, which further cloud the right answer for our relationship—or at least cue the shame around our choices.

It is so easy to base our decisions on what the standard is for other people around us, kind of a follow-the-crowd mentality. Does everyone around you have a house, kids, and a seemingly happy marriage? Does everyone else get to stay home, spend time volunteering, go to midmorning women's groups, and drop off and pick up their own kids?

When we compare, we lose sight of who we really are and what we really want. I'm not implying you will change your mind about what you want, but you will be able to drop the guilt and shame around your life being different from everyone else's (or at least what you perceive their life to be.) My goal is that you will not only let go of those feelings of guilt and shame, but that you will also actually be proud of the things that make your life different, and you will be able to see how they are unique adventures designed specifically for you.

When you know how to identify and debunk those outside voices, you'll gain your power back—and with power comes clarity. Even if your relationship status doesn't change, your paradigm will, giving you more confidence and trust in yourself, and you'll be able to witness how that, in turn, literally changes your situation. A clear mindset is the best place to hear Spirit-led inner guidance. Growing up in a Christian home, I was taught that "God is a spirit and has not a body like men" (gold star to me for still being able to quote Presbyterian catechism; see John 4:24 and II Corinthians 3:17). But that doesn't mean that God does not speak to us through our bodies. In fact, the deeper I dive into my neuroscience studies, the more I learn just how connected our bodies are to our emotions and subconscious thoughts.

Let me give you a more lighthearted example. I once dated a guy who was so stinking nice, you would've thought he was perfect. But every time we went out, I got a wave of nausea, seriously that "find a focal point and breathe through your nose" kind of nausea. I fought through it, thinking I was just nervous. I mean, he was so nice, and there were no red flags. In fact, I named him Vanilla Steve (not to his face, of course) because he was so consistent and had zero surprises.

So, I kept explaining away the feeling I thought was just nerves—until I shushed the impostor voices in my head that argued, "This guy is so nice. Why would you not want to date this guy?" After trying for months to explain away the nausea, I realized my intuition was screaming at me through my body, "This is not the guy for you!"

Sure, dating nerves are real, and although they are not always intuition, they *are* always related to impostor voices (maybe telling you that you are not good enough or you are not worthy or that you should be the person you think this guy will like). I was so relieved and so confident in my decision to stop seeing Vanilla Steve once I realized my system was screaming, "Stop!"

In this book, I am going to help you tap into your intuition—that deep inner knowingness that is strong and clear—so that you can hear the voice of the Spirit clearly, whether it comes through a physical feeling or not. Igniting your intuition starts with the ability to get quiet and listen, really listen, to what comes up—the thing that wants your attention, the first thing that pops into your head—without explaining it away.

There are going to be emotions that float to the surface that you will have to work through. They are working for you, not against you, I promise. If there is fear, you will be able to acknowledge it, find the source, and address it head-on. If there is grief, you will be able to allow yourself to feel it. You have to walk through your emotions to get to the other side. So many of us women are so good at shoving our emotions down or taking that emotional energy and dumping it into a good cause. But if we don't face our emotions and work with them, we cannot really hear our intuition. The voice of the Spirit gets warped by those feelings that we are trying not to feel.

It may feel impossible now, but you will have all the tools you need to create a life that you love, whether it is with your current partner or without. Often, identifying the impostor voices of expectations and comparisons resets your perspective of your relationship—and your perspective of yourself. Listening to your intuition opens up the pathway for the Spirit to guide you to the right decision. No matter what your conclusion, you will have the tools you need to own your story and allow it to propel you forward into a successful, fulfilling future.

Wouldn't it be nice if you had a book that told you exactly what to do? The beauty of crowdsourcing your answers is that someone (or a lot of someones) tells you what to do. But that is not the way to a Spirit-led decision. The tools to making Spirit-led decisions, if practiced, become habits—and before you know it, you'll be following inner guidance like it's second nature.

If you are open and willing to do the work, here is what you can expect: You will be able to end the blame game and take responsibility for your choices, which is ultimately going to shift your relationship. You will know how to identify impostor voices like comparisons and expectations (which fling open the door for fear and self-doubt to come in), so you can hear your answers clearly and trust your decisions more. You'll have a proven method to help you stop comparing yourself and your life to others, which will empower you to be more yourself and proud of it, giving you an identity outside of your relationship or marriage. You'll be able to sort through outside influences to discover what is truly in your heart, and you'll be keenly aware of the inner guidance speaking to you through your intuition—a recipe for a decision you can feel good about. You will be able to use your intuitive skills to uncover the best conclusion for your children—or your future children.

I feel confident that, by the end of this book, you will feel empowered to create a life you love through decisions you feel confident in. You already have the power to own your story and use it to inspire others, in ways big or small, even if your current relationship has not turned out to be what you planned.

Quietly communing with God, when we are searching for guidance, is a way of temporarily turning off our ego-mind [that says] 'I can fix this' . . . When you practice communing quietly with spirit, you will sense the presence of a sacred partner.

— DR. WAYNE DYER

Expectations are everywhere. We can't escape them, but the more we are aware of them, the better we can quiet the outside noise and hear our inner voice.

How do you become aware of the expectations surrounding you? Pull out that pen and journal. When you write your thoughts down, you become more aware of them. That's why, even without a photographic memory, making a grocery list helps you remember things, even if you don't look at it while you shop. (Full disclosure on the grocery list front: I still have to look at mine. There's always that one thing I forget!)

Your expectations of yourself are probably clouded by everyone else's expectations of you right now. So, we are going to save that category of expectations and start with your expectations of the relationship. When you said yes to commitment—when you envisioned this life you would create together—what did you see? Write those visions down. There are probably many, but make sure you get at least ten onto the page, and don't discard expectations that you might consider obvious for a relationship. Here are some examples to get your juices flowing:

- I envisioned merging our finances.
- I envisioned having kids together.
- I envisioned being a stay-at-home mom after having kids.
- I envisioned having dinner ready every evening when he came home from work.
- I envisioned family vacations together.
- I envisioned going to church as a family.
- I envisioned working out together a couple of times each week.

Some of these might spark others for you, and that's the idea. If you are in a groove, keep going. If you've hit a block, come back to this exercise later, maybe even after you've had a chance to take a walk and clear your head a little bit.

Take a look at your list. If you replace "envisioned" with "expected," you've got a list of the expectations you have for your relationship. Here is where the waters get muddy—what would your partner's list of expectations look like? We often assume our expectations match our partner's, especially if wedding bells are ringing in our future (even with the best premarital counseling).

I'm not going to make you do this, but I bet you would find it helpful to flip a journal page and make a list of what you think your partner's expectations were at the onset of the relationship (or even after a major point of commitment).

I'm not going to pretend I can get inside a man's head, but I can think of several examples where the top of the partner's list would be "I expect her to support my dreams, no matter the sacrifice." For some, this means going back to work after you have kids and being the breadwinner for a while so that he can get his own business started. For others, this means raising kids alone most of the time because he is working long hours, on the road, or even deployed.

Sit with these expectations for a while. Mull them over. Journal about them. Revisit them later this week. Let them sink in. Maybe this is the fault line in your relationship. Maybe you can work together and bridge that gap, resetting both parties' expectations together. Realizing what your expectations are of the relationship and how they differ from your partner's might be the first step to reconciliation. Even if reconciliation is not the cards for your relationship, being aware of these expectations is the first step in making a Spirit-led decision.

There is a difference between expectations and agreements. Let me say that again: There is a difference between expectations and agreements. That realization was a major aha moment for me. You and your partner may have had different expectations of your relationship, but you also might have had some agreements. These are things that you both talked about, that you at least verbally agreed on. It's a good idea to get these on the table too. If you want to, write them down, and also note which were actually verbally agreed on.

Let's take a really obvious example: fidelity. You would think that should be a given, but it never hurts to agree on everything. In his vows, my ex wrote that he would bring me coffee every day. That man, despite all his other failures, brought me coffee every day, even when he was cheating on me. (Of course, I would rather get my own coffee and be in a monogamous marriage—but when it came to that agreement, he kept it.)

Yes, relationships change over time. You might

not need or want the same things now that you did twenty years ago, or even three years ago. Agreements can change too, but the key is to change them together, to be intentional about them and make sure that both parties truly agree.

Another difference to look at while we're sorting out expectations and agreements is fault versus responsibility. You might be in a relationship where those verbal agreements (as opposed to your unspoken expectations—again, it's important to be very clear about these two) have not been met, and there is no sign in sight of the situation getting sorted out. The act of realizing your expectations of your relationship—and the fact that your partner might have entered the relationship with different expectations—pumps the brakes on the blame game that we so easily get caught up in. Even with differing expectations, you have to decide whether you will be able to meet in the middle and get on the same page with new agreements. Maybe his expectations have changed. Maybe your expectations have changed. Maybe there are original agreements that have not been (or are no longer being) met. These are all things to consider in your decision, but the one thing, oh so closely related to all of these, that will not move you forward and will drown out clarity in a heartbeat is the blame game.

There is likely a lot of fault lurking in your broken relationship. Fault and the feelings it brings up are worthy of acknowledgment. It's okay to recognize that your expectations have not been met, that agreements have been broken. It's okay to feel hurt and sad and to grieve, but it's not okay to hang out in blame. Really, it doesn't feel good there anyway. If you catch yourself thinking (or saying to your friends) "because he . . . ," take a deep breath, repeat the statement, acknowledge the feelings it brings up, and let it go. Yes, it is probably a true statement. Even though someone is at fault, you still have a responsibility to yourself to move forward, whether it is together or separately. Hanging out on the edge of the cliff of blame will send your dreams and the most vibrant parts of you tumbling into the abyss. You will not be able to make the best decision for you if it is blurred with blame.

MEETING OTHERS' EXPECTATIONS

Vishen Lakhiani is a mindfulness teacher whose work I find to be real and down-to-earth. In his book *The Code of the Extraordinary Mind,* he introduces the idea of "brules." The "b" in front of "rules" stands for bullshit. Let's say it all together: bullshit rules! How many of us are living and making our decisions based on brules that have been put on us? Brules come in many forms: limiting beliefs, societal norms, parental expectations; the list goes on.

Brules can be hard to bring to the surface because some of them are so ingrained in us, we don't even notice them anymore or we view them as absolute truth. In Claire's well-educated family, a common brule was that you have to get a four-year college degree to be successful. Where she grew up, this was a fact just as plain and simple as "the sky is blue." Being super artistic, she knew that she wouldn't fit in or be happy pursuing a four-year degree to study something that wouldn't be part of her future anyway. She broke the mold and went to cosmetology school instead. Tossing out that brule was painful for Claire. She felt like she disappointed a lot of well-meaning people whom she loved, but now she makes great money doing something that she's passionate about.

By identifying and being aware of the brules that govern our lives, we can move forward in multiple ways. We can toss out generational beliefs that are untrue but have still been ruling our families. We can identify expectations placed on us by other people and by society that don't align with our own dreams or who God truly made us to be. We can get back to the core of who we really are and quiet those outside voices so we can hear Spirit clearly.

Wrestling with brules is a beast, but we're going to walk through it together, step by step.

Let's start with ten things you believe about yourself or your role in the relationship. (Deep breath, you can do it. I make my clients start with thirty, so I'm going easy on you.) In a more general exercise, these beliefs can be either positive or negative, but for the sake of this life-altering decision and quieting the outside influences and expectations, let's make this list one of beliefs that you perceive to be negative.

Here are some examples to get the ball rolling:

- I'm a terrible housekeeper (because I work all the time).
- I'm not sexy/physically attractive unless I weigh _____.
- I can't be a good mom if I work full time.
- I'm not capable of making my own money.
- Just being myself isn't good enough.
- I have to accomplish a lot to be valuable.
- To be a good mom and wife, I have to make sacrifices. Choosing what I want is selfish.

You might be realizing how easy it is to come up with thirty!

Remember, these are beliefs. We are going to dig into these to find the brules behind them. If you can do more than ten, keep going. If you feel like ten is a good stopping place for now, move on to the next step. Either way, I encourage you to keep this exercise going. It's a powerful habit to address your beliefs and face them head-on. Jotting down about two to five beliefs in your journal each day—and doing the following exercise on them—can completely shift your life. And guess what? It is also the path to making Spirit-led decisions.

The second step of this exercise is to identify where you picked up each of these beliefs. Take one at a time, starting with the one that elicits the most pressure or emotion, and ask yourself the following questions about that belief:

- Where did you first pick it up?
- How old were you?
- Where did it come from (Mom, Dad, someone else)?
- Describe the exact moment. Can you remember what you were wearing at that moment?

The more detail you can remember and write down, the more powerful this exercise will be. Recalling detail fires up those neural pathways and allows us to address the root of the belief. Identifying the origin of this brule will help you break it down and see it for what it is: an outside influence that created a storyline for you to hold on to. It likely had a good reason to stick around, but one that you might not need anymore.

One of the brules that ruled my life for a long time was that you can't do what you love and make a good living. I thought I had to choose. I didn't think being in love with my work and making a great living was a possibility. As I worked through this belief, I was able to envision exactly the moment I picked it up. I was about six years old, standing in the living room of my childhood home. My parents were in the dining room, just on the other side of the sofa, arguing about my mother going back to work. They had each given up their dreams for each other. My dad had given up his career in music to be more present with our family, and my mom was giving up her dream of staying at home with the kids to go back to nursing and bring in a stable income. In that moment, my little brain created that brule. It was well-intentioned—at that moment in time, it kept our family together and stable, something that's important to a six-year-old—but my adult self doesn't need that brule. My adult self is not in the same boat and is absolutely capable of making a great living doing what I love.

Identifying the brules that possess so much influence over your life, even if they don't seem like they are directly related to your relationship, is going to help this decision become so clear. This is a huge part of quieting those outside voices, and in the process, you might realize there are expectations of your relationship that are not your own and that some expectations may have been put in place to appease other people. Some brules creep in because we are comparing ourselves to others. We want to have what everyone else has, even if it is not one of our core values. Material possessions are a great example here. Have you ever felt like you are less successful because the car you drive is different from what your friends have or because you live in a different part of town? Have you stopped to ask yourself if those things are what you really want or if you just want them in order to lump yourself in with people you admire?

In her mid-thirties, Sarah found herself in a strange place in life—suddenly single again, yet she had toned down the pursuit of her career to pursue a better family life. (I can certainly relate! Can you?)

She wasn't driving the luxury cars that her friends who had just focused on career were driving, nor was she driving the Tahoe that her soccer mom friends were driving. She was no longer living in a house in the 'burbs, and her relationship had set back her savings, so she couldn't buy a townhome in the city. It was this strange in-between place, and she let it make her feel bad about herself for a while. "If I would have just stayed the course and not taken the risk on a relationship . . ." she would tell me, then she "wouldn't be behind." Through much conversation and contemplation, though, she realized that she actually loved her little apartment in the city and her Jeep. (Okay, my Jeep bias might have helped swing it a little.) All of a sudden, she was aware that she was not only right where she needed to be, but right where she *wanted* to be.

So many psychologists and behavior experts out there have studies indicating that we all have our own set of values that we live by, see the world through, and base our judgments on. The problem with this undeniable fact is that everyone else is living by their own set of values. Yet so often we expect others to live by, see the world through, and base judgments on *our* values—and they hold the same expectation of us based on *their* values. Sounds extremely stressful, doesn't it? Trying to live up to these expectations actually makes our own core values extremely gray, so much so that sometimes we don't even know what our own core values are.

One of my favorite experts on this subject, Dr. John Demartini, teaches that your top values are what you spend the majority of your time doing, where your thoughts go most often, what takes up space in your home and your world, and what you spend your money on. You can take his values determination quiz at drdemartini.com/values. It is completely acceptable to live by your own core values and for your partner to live by theirs. In fact, it's enlightening and even liberating to realize what your top values are and to welcome them into your life with open arms.

Take a look back at your list of expectations of your relationship, then take a look back at your list of brules. Are any of these expectations based on someone else's top values? If they are not aligned with your top values, it's time to toss them out!

Let me remind you of something that is so, so important to remember throughout this book, throughout this process, and throughout life: you were put on this earth to be *you*. You might be familiar with the scripture verse that says you are wonderfully made, Psalm 139:14. Don't you think that God created you, your passions, and your top values to be a unique part of this world? Your values are valid. You are worthy of living by the values and passions that God placed in you, not the top values designed for someone else.

It is so easy to get caught up in the belief that if someone is not living by our top values, they are wrong. We get stubborn and don't believe there is any other way. And sometimes we are even the victims in that scenario—making ourselves squeeze into someone else's top values in order to avoid judgment and be perceived as in the right.

I think that often when we are living by others' expectations, it's easy to get caught up in what God wants *from* us instead of what God wants *for* us. God is much less concerned with you keeping the brules than he is with you being true to the values and passions that he intentionally designed and placed in you.

We've talked about your expectations of your relationship and we've talked about society's (or your family's or community's) expectations of you, but what about your expectations of yourself? Once you shove out the brules and others' expectations, what is left? Pull out that journal and make a list. What standards have you set for yourself? (You might see some of these parallel the list of ten to thirty beliefs you hold about yourself. Use that list as a cheat sheet for this exercise.) Do these expectations match your top core values? The next step with this list is one that can be hard to face: How many of these expectations of yourself are based on fear? Fear of failure? Fear of disappointing others? Fear of not being enough? Ouch. I know.

Underneath each expectation, write down the underlying fear, if there is one. Is it that you won't meet someone else's expectations of you? That you won't measure up? That you won't fit in? Ahhh, see how we're coming back to brules here. If your expectations of yourself are there to make sure you align with *someone else's* top values, it's time to toss them out. (Just realizing that they are not part of your own values will help you eliminate them.) It is totally fine and good to have expectations of yourself and to set standards, but make sure these expectations are based on your own top values, not somebody else's, and certainly not on brules.

Expectations of ourselves keep us on track, and as long as they align with our top values, they're not in the way. When you identify an expectation (whether it is physically written down or not), ask yourself *why* you have that expectation of yourself and follow the thread.

I'm going to write you a big fat permission slip here: You are allowed to want what you want! Sure, you might have to make some compromises along the way, but do not feel guilty about the desires of your heart.

This chapter has given you a lot to sort through. Sit with it. Work through these exercises. When "everyone else" is shouting what they want for you (even if they mean well), it sure makes it hard to hear that true inner, authentic guidance. You see, the Spirit whispers from that voice within you. So, make sure you've at least muffled the other voices shouting at you before you move on.

In the Bible, there's a story of a man named Elijah. His experience brings wisdom to us in I Kings 19:11–12, which says:

> *The Lord said, 'Go out and stand on the mountain in the presence of the Lord for the Lord is about to pass by.' Then a great powerful wind tore the mountains apart and shattered the rocks before the Lord, but the Lord was not in the wind. After the wind there was an earthquake, but the Lord was not in the earthquake. After the earthquake came a fire, but the Lord was not in the fire. And after the fire came a gentle whisper.* (NIV)

Not everyone struggles with perfectionism. I've always been a little jealous of my friends who never worry what anyone else thinks and never care if they get something exactly right. You know, the friends who aren't afraid to swing and miss. In fact, my fear of failure has stopped me from so many things—because I was afraid to swing and miss. The thought of not getting it right can be so embarrassing. And I know I am not alone. So, in an effort to save ourselves the embarrassment, we don't try, we don't take a risk, or worse, we try and then we try to hide our failure, acting like everything is okay or even like we meant for our attempt to turn out this way. Let's be honest. I never throw my cookies in the oven wanting them to come out burned to a crisp, but sometimes (okay, most times) they do!

Life can feel that way too. You never walk down the aisle expecting it to end in divorce. You also don't expect infidelity, abuse, or even just disappointment to creep into a relationship, but they do. And here you are at this crossroads, trying to sort it all out, and probably feeling bad about even considering leaving. On top of it all, if you're human, you've probably tried to cover up that it's falling apart or starting to fray.

Perfectionism stems from a habit (maybe even a generational habit) of comparison. *Ugh, no! I'm totally secure in myself and I don't compare my life to others.* I hear you—except that we all do. Let me say that again: we all do.

Comparison is not all bad. It helps us set standards and allows us to strive to reach the next level. When it turns sour is when we feel discontent with our uniqueness or the uniqueness of our story because we want what someone else has—someone else's lifestyle, someone else's house, someone else's abs! We are uniquely made in body and in life.

You were not put on this earth to live a life that someone else is already living. It's okay to want two and a half kids, a goldendoodle, and a house with a white picket fence. It's not okay to want those things just because they're what everyone else has or what everyone (or anyone) else thinks you should have.

I remember catching up with a childhood friend in my mid-twenties. I had already been through one divorce, and she was fairly newly married (maybe two or three years in). In our catch-up, she described to me that she was taking off to California to pursue an acting career. Just for the record, this was not a whim; she actually did already have a successful career in acting and modeling, but she felt a move to the West Coast would take her to the next level. And her husband was staying in Tennessee. They had plans to see each other every couple of months, and they were both totally happy and in agreement about that decision. That led us into a conversation about the standards society has set around marriage—or maybe not even society, maybe just our parents or the community we grew up in. What my friend and her husband were doing was totally outside the box, and everyone seemed to be a little shocked and maybe even secretly expected them to fail. But they didn't. For several years they made it work, and when the time was right, she moved back to Tennessee. Now, nearly two decades later, they have two adorable kids. (She posts the most hilarious mom-stories on social media.) And yes, she still has a successful marriage and acting career.

What if they had decided they had to play by the brules? What if she decided that her dreams were not worth risking everyone else's judgment? (See what I mean about being jealous of my friends who don't care? Haha.) Yet, out of all of the amazing couples I know, she and her husband are the only ones I can think of who have a story like that—a story where they broke the brules to foster each other's dreams. They weren't worried about measuring up to everyone else's standard of a perfect marriage.

It's tempting to let comparison set the standard for our lives (in whatever area) instead of setting that standard according to our inner guidance, our desires, and our dreams. That is where the perfectionism bug will creep in, take over your mind, hijack your life, and make you miserable.

Identifying the comparisons we make is a heck of a lot easier than dropping the habit of comparing.

Journal time! Grab that pen. Write down the first ten comparisons that come to mind that have dictated the standards you've set for your life. We're going to follow these up with some hard questions, so leave a couple lines of space between each of them. (And no cheating—make your list first before you get to the follow-up questions!)

Once you've got your list of ten, ask yourself:

Is this a standard you want in your life?

If yes, *why?* Why do you want that? Are you trying to validate a belief you hold about yourself? Is it the result of an unnecessary expectation or a comparison? Or is it really, truly a desire of your heart?

Let me give you an example. In my twenties, I worked in the fitness industry, and when my first marriage ended, I started doing fitness competitions. I'd mentioned my interest in these competitions to my ex while we were married, and verbatim, his response was, "Oh sweetheart, you'll never be good enough to do that." So naturally, the first thing I did when we split was sign up for a competition and hit the gym. (You might think that's the lesson in this story. Yes, I was seeking validation to debunk a belief that he planted that I was not good enough—but that's not actually where I'm going with this. Stick with me.)

For five years, I trained most of the time, and even when I wasn't working toward a competition on the calendar, I was training and eating like I was getting ready for the stage. They say it takes twenty-one days to build a habit. Well, over the course of five years, that's a lot of cycles of twenty-one days drilling into my head that I have to be 10 percent body fat in order to be worthy.

The fitness competition stage is comparison and perfectionism bootcamp. Yes, yes, I was 10 percent body fat on that stage. From the time I got divorced to the time I stepped on a competition stage for the first time (nine months later), I dropped forty pounds and reduced my body fat by more than half—and I looked amazing. But guess what? My participation continually enforced the message that I still didn't look as good as the girl who got first place. Show after show, my perception that I wasn't good enough was reinforced (even in third place; it's not like I was coming in last, y'all!).

During this time, I was also getting a lot of attention off the stage for the way I looked. Personal training clients at the gym wanted to work with me. They'd seen me do for myself what they were trying to achieve. So I was learning that even off the stage, I needed to look a certain way all the time to be good enough: to make enough money, to attract the good-looking men, to be noticed at the gym. Now, nearly twenty years later, and having spent the last decade working toward a healthy balance, I still find myself comparing the way I look to the other women in the gym. Usually I don't even catch the thought until I feel the feeling that the thought creates (guilt, shame, "I'm not good enough").

By making a list of comparisons that you

commonly depend on, you are calling them out, and you're also identifying thought patterns. When we identify thought patterns, we can shift the comparison— and, drumroll, delete it!

Comparisons aren't always just general ideas or concepts; sometimes (and for some of us, most of the time) the comparison is to a specific person. Maybe it's your best friend, maybe a sister, maybe someone at work, or even an archenemy from the present or past.

There is a ton of research out there on the neuroplasticity of the brain and how you can actually change your brain by changing thought patterns. To tackle comparisons, I like to use a technique that rewires the paths in your brain by calling up very specific memories and recognizing that the characteristics that you admire in someone else also exist in yourself. Let's distill this into a journal exercise to get you started.

If you're comparing yourself to someone else, you have them on a pedestal of some sort, even if you don't want to admit it. In one or more areas of life, you think that this person is better than you. Take out that pen. It's journal time.

There very well may be more than one of these people, but for the sake of this exercise, just choose one. Write down at least five characteristics you like about this person, leaving several lines of space between each.

Now, we are going to bring up specific memories of when you saw that person exhibit each characteristic. *Very* specific, like we did with the memories around your beliefs about yourself. While we are not going to write out each whole memory, I do want you to write down when each memory took place. Next to the time, write down where you were (it's okay to use shorthand, but it is important to actually write rather than type). Now completely go to that moment in time in your mind, writing down key words and details about that memory. Be specific; if the person was wearing a pineapple shirt, make sure "pineapple shirt" gets on the page. Include specific feelings that come up, both significant emotions and feelings in your body. Be present in that moment while you call up this memory. You can pile the words on top of one another. It might look like chicken scratch, and that's okay. The act of writing helps your brain call up the specifics and create new pathways. Follow this process for each of the five characteristics.

Once you have the memories of that person written out, I want you to follow the same process to recall specific times where *you* have demonstrated that characteristic. Do this for each of the five characteristics. The memories you recall this time don't have to be memories with that person, just any memories in which you exhibited that characteristic that you admire. If you struggle to recall a memory, wait for it; take some deep breaths, maybe even take a walk. It is there and will come up, I promise!

When this exercise is complete (and it's not a quick and easy one), you should be able to see—and really deeply feel—that these characteristics that you have idolized in another person also exist in you.

Karen was always comparing herself to Leslie. Leslie seemed to have it all together, and her Instagram feed certainly reinforced that idea. She and her kids always looked cute—never like terrors making horrid fashion statements in the middle of Target. She sent the kids off to unique day camps all summer, while she got her workouts in and made dinners from scratch. Leslie seemed to be perfectly happy in her perfect world. Karen thought if she could meal prep and plan her kids' activities (empowered by the latest Erin Condren planner) like Leslie did, she could be a better mom, but her financial resources were limited. She couldn't afford to send her kids off to all the camps or shop at Whole Foods for rare ingredients that she would only use for a single recipe. She let these limitations influence her self-worth as a mom and set expectations that really didn't belong in her life or her relationship.

Karen was deeply creative. She loved her garden, and her kids loved watching the veggies and herbs they planted grow and then learning how to cook with them. Her kids were always creating something, and she was always finding family activities out in nature or at the library (the long-lost Mecca of free and fun activities). Once Karen realized that her kids were getting a different but immensely valuable experience, she was able to see her worth as a mom and reset her expectation of herself and of her marriage.

What does that have to do with making a Spirit-led decision about your relationship? Often the people in our lives whom we hold in the highest esteem influence our decisions the most. Comparing yourself and your life to those people can create noise that muffles the sound of true guidance and creates confusion.

Leveling the playing field isn't just about bringing the people you have on a pedestal down—it's also about raising yourself up. This is where the fun begins. This is one of my favorite things to teach because I am so passionate about it.

There is no one in this world just like you. For some reason, it is pretty easy to accept that about our physical bodies, at least the parts we can't change. We know that our DNA is different. We know we each have a different fingerprint—and not just out of the 8 billion people in the world right now, but even out of everyone who has ever lived.

If we take it to the next level, we see that our personalities are unique too. There are so many personality assessments out there: Myers-Briggs, Enneagram, the list goes on. And really, I don't know anyone who doesn't enjoy reading the results. (Shout-out to the guys who created them for empowering us by pointing out the strengths and uniqueness of our personalities!)

But when we dig even deeper, we get to our lives, our actual day-to-day, and our journey—our stories. No one was put on this earth to live the exact same life that was mapped out for you. Although there will be similarities along the way—experiences that help us build bonds and support each other—your life and your story are uniquely yours. So why do we work so hard to keep up with the Joneses and fit in the mold? Yep, you know it: We let comparison get the best of us. Then our old friend perfectionism sneaks in. Then the guilt of not measuring up (guilt of being different—ouch!) starts navigating for us. And before we know it, fear of failure is in the driver's seat.

I don't know about you, but in my car, that fear of failure guy blasts the radio so loud I can't even hear my own thoughts. I've never known the Spirit or my inner voice to lead by shouting, so let's kick the loud guys out of the car so we can hear the whisper.

We've covered a lot of abstract ground, so let me break down the main takeaways for you:

- Comparison leads to perfectionism, which leads to fear of failure.
- Comparison can stem from society, brules, or overvaluing another individual.
- Debunk comparison by noticing it, acknowledging it, and identifying the belief that is supporting it. (You know how to debunk those beliefs and brules from the work you did in chapter 4.)
- Bring individuals that you hold in high esteem down from the pedestal by recognizing that the same qualities that you admire in them also exist in you.

The activities in this chapter involve a lot of internal work, but that doesn't mean the concepts don't appear more tangibly in life.

My mom was a working mom, and she was always comparing herself to the moms who didn't have to work. Even in my thirties, she would still ask, "Was I a bad mom for working?" and the answer was always an emphatic, "No, Mom!" with a little laugh (because I'd answered that question the same way a million times before). You see, if she had written down the characteristics of those stay-at-home moms that she idolized, she would have also been able to identify times that she exhibited those same characteristics herself. What better way to make it clear just what a wonderful mom she was?

Maybe your perfectionism is a by-product of strict parents or parents who wanted what they really felt was best for you. You might need to dig a little deeper to figure out if your perfectionism is rooted in expectations or if it stems from someone you put on a pedestal. It might even be a little bit of both. Either way, you have the tools and exercises to work through it.

I remember trying to explain that I was a personal trainer to my grandad, who was in his eighties at the time. He was a farmer and busi-nessman with several investments. He held positions on numerous boards in town, like the bank and the hospital. He was successful—in a very traditional sense. Sitting next to me on the sofa after Sunday lunch, he had a million questions about personal training. What hours did I work? Was it Monday through Friday? Why would anyone pay money for someone else to tell them how to exercise? (Farmer, remember?) What did I do with my time between 1:00 p.m. and 3:00 p.m. when people weren't exercising?

I felt like I was being grilled—and with every question, I felt like I wasn't living up to his standard of success. When I removed all of my assumptions from that situation, though, like that he wouldn't see me as successful unless my success looked like his, I could see that he was asking all of these questions not to make a judgment about my job, but because he wanted to understand it. In that moment, I was so busy comparing myself to him that I missed his point completely.

Okay, I just have to tell you one more Grandad story, because I feel like our relationship is a great example of how we build people up in our minds and hold ourselves to standards that aren't even there. He left this earth just about six months before I started writing the first edition of this book. When I got the call that he had chosen hospice, I booked the next flight out of Texas and headed to Tennessee. Since I was his first grandchild, we had a special bond, and I was not about to let him slip out of this realm without holding my hand one last time.

We had a lot of special moments that weekend

and even several hours all to ourselves. I had something weighing on me, additional grief, and I felt like he needed to know. I expected some backlash, but what did I have to lose? Over the previous three years, I had been on a journey to become a Single Mother by Choice. I had transferred my first embryo a few weeks before Grandad went into the hospital, but my embryo didn't stick. It was a girl, and there was no medical explanation for the loss, but my heart hurt terribly, and I needed the kind of bear hug that only a grandad can give.

I thought that he would be concerned about me being a single mother; I thought he would be worried about what other people would think if I were pregnant and unmarried. But I told him anyway. Again, he asked a million questions. He even asked me to explain the science behind IVF (in vitro fertilization). As I did, his face lit up with the biggest grin and, with a laugh, he said, "If anyone is going to figure out how to make a family on her own, it's going to be Ginny Ellsworth." It was at that moment that I realized that all of those times that he was asking a million questions, it wasn't because he was judging me—it was because he was proud of me.

We are so good at making assumptions and creating stories in our minds about what everyone else thinks of us, about what that means about us and our worth. Embrace the internal work that will set you free, and tell those impostors to hush. Maya Angelou said it best:

> *You alone are enough. You have nothing to prove to anybody.*

# FINDING THE WOMAN WHO GOT LOST IN THE SHUFFLE

We've hung out quite a bit with some really tough topics so far. While completely necessary for making a Spirit-led decision and in the end liberating and empowering, the exercises we've covered so far can be draining. So, I'm happy to bring you into a space that is more fun to work with and just as important: *you*.

God absolutely sends guidance through signs and other people, but the primary voice that the Spirit uses is actually already inside you. However, many of us have been trained to ignore it, or we hear it but quickly dismiss it. So far, we've sorted through a bunch of junk—other people's expectations, your own expectations—and determined which of those were founded on made-up rules, comparisons, etc. We've even touched on how your life is uniquely yours. Now that all of that is out of the way, let's look inside you.

You are "fearfully and wonderfully made," you "know that full well," right? (Psalm 139:14, NIV).

Take a minute to be still. Take a few slow, deep breaths and let your mind drift back to childhood. Before all the impostor voices came in, what did you most enjoy in life? What did you imagine your life would look like when you grew up?

I completely realize that many children aren't aware of all the possibilities that life has to offer, so let's bring that inner child to the present. Knowing what you know now, without all the clutter, what do you want your life to look like?

Don't worry, I am not going to tell you to chuck your relationship in the trash and go get that ideal life that you wanted. (Okay, I'm probably going to encourage you to go get the life you want, but not necessarily to chuck your relationship. This decision is a process!) This exercise is about recognizing your inner desires—the things in life that light you up. This is about getting in touch with who you really are and honoring that woman.

I remember sitting around a big table on the evening of Valentine's Day with my girls' Bible study group. We were in seventh or eighth grade, still young. As a fun Valentine's Day conversation, our leader had us go around the table and take a guess at how old we thought we would be when we got married and how many kids we thought we would have. Sure, it sounds harmless and fun, but the assumption was that each of us would fit the mold that society and the church expected us to fill. Having never given either of those much thought, I said I thought I would be twenty-six and have three kids. Right there, y'all, I verbalized those expectations and they stuck. When I had the chance to get married at the age of twenty (he proposed when I was eighteen, yikes), I thought I had to say yes because I was supposed to follow the plan. So no wonder, when it didn't work out, I felt like a failure. (For the record, I said "I don't know" when he first asked me to marry him, but by the time he officially proposed, I'd been convinced to say yes, by both him and my own logic.)

Had I been more in touch with myself and what I wanted (and my inner wisdom), I would not have made the decision that I made. I would have realized that I actually was totally fine not being married by twenty-six or having three kids! As an adult (which really quite literally wasn't until after that marriage), I began learning more about myself and what makes me *me*—my strengths, my weaknesses—and even learning to love those and the uniqueness they bring. A partner, kids, and a house don't make you unique; *you* make you unique.

So, before we pull the trigger on your big decision, let's dig deeper into who you are and what you want in life. The challenge in this exercise is to set aside the expectations you have of your relationship, especially the ones that have not been met. You cannot base what you want on what you do not have. So, if you need to take some time to process the previous chapters further, please do.

Remember that list of negative beliefs you have (or at this point, maybe "had") about yourself? Now, pull out that journal and make a list of thirty positive beliefs you have about yourself. If you feel up to it, follow the same steps of identifying where those beliefs came from. (You might be surprised to find some intruders in there too.)

Take a minute or two to send those moments (or people) in your life some gratitude! Did you know there is a vibrational scale of emotions? While I'm not going to get into the details here, I will tell you that gratitude carries a high vibration and makes you feel *good*. Allowing yourself to soak up and enjoy those high vibrational feelings will also bring clarity to the voice of the Spirit and a sense of confidence to your decision.

While we are in this high vibrational level, I want you to make a list of the things you are grateful for in your relationship and about your partner. I'm not going to give you a certain number or a limit. We are not going to make a pros and cons list, but you can send some gratitude to the positive things that are present in your life and relationship.

My mother's constant internal struggle with my dad was his serial entrepreneurship. (He was and still is a sucker for a start-up!) It was a quality about him that she admired and loathed all at the same time. She carried resentment about having to go back to work after my brother and I were born, but she was acutely aware that no one—and I mean *no one*—would love her with the reckless abandon that my father did.

I remember several conversations where she struggled with being tired of being the source of stable benefits and questioned whether staying was right for her. But Mom was able to shift her mindset by recognizing what she had. Even though her life did not look the way she had envisioned, she took what she had and created opportunities for herself.

She felt like a bad mother and a bad Christian because she had to return to work. Because nurses often have strange hours, she was not at church every time the doors were open like she thought she should be. But she found a way to serve in, arguably, a more impactful way. God used who she was exactly where she was.

The line for visitation at her funeral was four hours long—and people waited. There were several people there who I had never met before, but she had touched their lives and they wanted to honor her life in return. Looking back, I vividly remember a lady approaching me (it is always a little terrifying, in the middle of such tremendous grief, to have to recognize people from childhood): "You don't know me," she said (phew, she let me off the hook), "but I worked at the same hospital as your mother, and every Friday for the past twenty-five years, she has been coming to my office and praying with me." *Whoa.*

Mom had never mentioned this lady. They didn't work in the same department. (Believe me, I knew everyone in that cardiac rehab department. They practically raised me.) Mom made a connection with this woman and diligently took the time to encourage her, an impact she would not have had if she had not gone back to work.

I share this story not to say that you should accept all of the things in life that aren't going according to plan, but to encourage you to look for those places where God is using you anyway, where God's plans were different from yours, even though these plans may not have been in your playbook. Stop for a minute and let that soak in. Maybe even take a minute to journal about it.

My mom's desires are not far from what so many women struggle with today. So many times I have heard, "I wanted to get married and have kids and stay home, but I also want financial freedom." She has a dream. He has a nice income (or a trust fund). While she might not marry him for money, she does have expectations. And some men want that too. I've dated men (okay, even married one) who tried to squish me into that box until they realized they were barking up the wrong tree.

It's important to keep your expectations in check, making sure they are realistic and beneficial for both of you. Sarah had an impeccable work ethic and was always hustling in her career. She got married expecting that she would have kids and build the business that she wanted *or* stay home if she wanted, but still have access to every bit of the family finances. The problem was that that was an expectation, not an agreement. She'd painted a picture in her mind of what their life would be like after the wedding (and even mentioned it to her partner), and when it didn't go according to her plan, resentment crept in (on both sides) and the romance, respect, and dedication faded.

The reality of the situation was that he was never going to give her full access to the finances that he brought in. She would never be able to be a stay-at-home mom with the husband-funded financial freedom that she wanted. Was she going to get what she wanted by leaving? No—but she wasn't going to get what she wanted by staying either. Either way, she was going to have to shift her expectations.

This example is not about the right versus the wrong way to handle finances in a relationship, but rather that navigating finances or anything else using expectations instead of agreements isn't going to get you where you want to go. If you have a partner-funded lifestyle, are you giving up something else that you want in exchange for that? If you do not have a partner-funded lifestyle but resent it, think about what you would realistically have to give up for that. Is that something you would be willing to do? When you shift out of expectations to agreements with your partner, be sure you are asking for something that is realistic and beneficial for both of you.

Sarah chose to leave and is now building a wildly successful business of her own. Sure, in her mind's eye the June Cleaver life would have been perfect, but in reality, she would have felt squashed in that relationship, even if she had access to every penny he brought in. Very important side note: money does not make you happy; you make you happy. So, let's get back to you . . .

I hope you can see how the exercises we've done so far can have a major impact in a circumstance like this. In order to make the best decision, you have got to quiet the outside voices. It is immensely personal to dig down deep and identify what you want in life and why. Is it an expectation of society or from someone else, or is it truly what your heart desires? You have to know the *why* in order for it to factor into your decision. If the why is attached to an expectation or a comparison, you have got to toss it out.

My friend Emily and I are always talking about the big life things, especially our growing businesses. She had me do an exercise that I'm probably going to adopt for my life, maybe even for each month. I drew a huge circle on a page in my journal. Inside it, I wrote everything I wanted in my life (tangible and intangible), and outside the circle, I wrote the things I did not want in my life. This could be a huge task, but even if you simplify it, it really makes you think! What do you really want in life? What makes you tick? What makes your heart throb? (Not what makes the Joneses raise an eyebrow or what makes your family give you a pat on the back.)

Take a moment and give it a try. Now look at your circle. Is your life facilitating the things inside your circle? Is it protecting you from the things outside the circle? Are there any shifts you could make to move toward having those things inside your circle and eliminating the things outside the circle?

From this chapter, I want you to have a clearer view of who you were made to be and what the desires of your heart truly are. If you want to be a stay-at-home mom because you think that is what good moms do (like my mom did), you've got to toss that factor out because it's based on an expectation. If you want to be a stay-at-home mom because that is truly your desire, and you'd want it even if no one else were on planet Earth (except you and your kids) and you didn't have anyone to impress, then you can factor that in. It's a God-given desire of your heart.

Let's talk about those God-given desires. When we are really in alignment with the Spirit and doing what God made us to do, it is super easy to lose track of time, which is a sneaky little trick to begin identifying those desires and passions. For me, it's when I am creating (on my values evaluation, creating is my highest value). For me, this includes writing, painting, and even cooking.

Let's press pause on this big agonizing decision and enjoy discovering your God-given passions and desires. This is the fun part! Pull out your journal. What are you inevitably doing that, if you don't have any other obligations, will whisk you away to a time-less dimension? Maybe it's creating. Maybe it's being social. Maybe it's teaching. Maybe it's being with your kids. What you discover might surprise you. As you brainstorm potential answers, you'll know you've got it right when you feel that life-sized smile spread across your face at just the thought of it. Have at least three, and if you have ten (or more), put a star next to three that you could work toward making time for in your life.

These things do not have to be taking up the majority of space in your life, but they do have to be present in your life for you to be fulfilled. For exam-ple, if painting lights you up and your partner isn't on board with you launching a painting business, that's not necessarily a reason to walk away. But if you don't have any sort of painting outlet in your life at all, figuring out a way to include it is important.

In my second marriage, I spent hours in the garage, where I kept old pallets, broke them up, and used them as canvases. (The magazine I was working for had copies delivered to the office, and I got first pick of the pallets before the old guy in a pickup truck came to scoop them up.) My ex would even come out and help me pull them apart. For being such a jerk, he had his "nice guy" moments. (Seriously, I think every woman in this decision struggles with the tug-of-war between what she likes about her partner and what is intolerable.) I wasn't looking to start a business or an Etsy shop. In fact, at the time, I didn't even realize that painting pallets fulfilled one of my highest values. But painting in my garage was a place where I completely lost track of time, and, despite a failing marriage, that desire still existed in my life. (Insert major gratitude for that moment!)

Let's take a moment to celebrate *you!* Take a look at your list and then consider what's inside your circle. How beautiful are these desires and passions that are so deeply rooted within you? What a unique gift you are to the world! Where are your deepest desires showing up in your life? Are any of them being blocked by your relationship?

Please don't take my above example to mean that if your abusive husband breaks up pallets for you to paint, it's a good enough reason to stay. It's not. *But* I hope that, so far, you have learned that you have so much to be proud of! I hope that you have identified areas where God is using you, even though your life might not look like what you think it should or even what you want. Maybe you have even seen how you actually are fulfilling some of your desires, your passions, and your purpose right where you are in life.

These desires play a bigger part in listening to the Spirit than just being pieces of the puzzle in your decision. Remember the vibrational scale I mentioned? When you are doing what you love, you vibrate with emotions at a higher level on the scale. Think back to thoughts that make you feel heavy and down. Those thoughts elicit emotions that vibrate at low levels. They are tied to expectations, brules, or untrue beliefs you have about yourself, aren't they? So, it's clear to see that when you are vibrating at higher levels, you feel closer to God, and it's easier to hear the voice of the Spirit, the whisper. The voices of the impostors quiet down.

God loves these things about you! He made them! That is why you vibrate (you can substitute "emote" if the metaphysics of vibration still feels foreign to you) closer to him when you are fulfilling these passions and desires.

I want to close this part of the conversation with a quote from one of my favorite hymns:

Could we with ink the ocean fill and were the skies of parchment made
    Were every stalk on earth a quill, and every man a scribe by trade
    To write the love of God above would drain the ocean dry,
    Nor could the scroll contain the whole though stretched from sky to sky.

— "THE LOVE OF GOD," F.M. LEHMAN

That is some big love, y'all.

As a Christian, I was taught different ways of connecting to God, the most common being prayer and worship. My high school was super artsy, and music was a way my fellow students and I really connected to God. I remember the presence of the Spirit being so strong at times that the air felt thick. Occasionally during worship, group prayer time, or even my own conversations with God (typically from my giant walk-in closet where I hibernated under the huge window that looked out at the field across the street), I would see visions—a fancy spiritual word given to mental images. I used to sing worship songs from my bed before I fell asleep, even at a very young age. I remember my dad coming to check on me one night because he heard noise coming from my room (I was trying to be quiet). Worship was my jam, even as a child.

I share this to tell you that I always knew I had, well, I won't call it an *unusual* but maybe an *atypical* way of connecting to God. Throughout adulthood, I would also have strange experiences like thinking of a person and then getting a call from them right after. For the longest time, I chalked it up to coincidence, but now I know that it was intuition. I didn't know much about intuition, just that occasionally I would get a gut feeling and would typically dismiss it or let my impostor voices logic it away. But intuition is in fact a strong way that God speaks to us and a clear way to get answers about your relationship.

Since then, I've learned how to ignite my intuition so I can more clearly recognize the voice of the Spirit, and it has dramatically changed my life. Because prayer and worship connect to God through the mind and soul, it was challenging for me to trust the connections I have to God with my body. *Embodiment* is a word that started popping up for me a few years ago, but I didn't really know what it meant. Embodiment is being connected to the feelings and sensations in your body. God created your body, not just your mind, and if we learn how to pay attention, we can get answers through our bodies, too.

In this chapter, I am going to teach you some easy practices to start recognizing when the Spirit speaks through your intuition using your mind and your body. I've got great news: you've already quieted the impostor voices—or at least learned to recognize them—which is a huge step in clearly hearing the Spirit's guidance!

John 14:17 reminds us that this voice is already in us: "the Spirit of truth . . . you know Him, for He dwells with you and will be in you" (NKJV).

There are simple things that you can add to your daily life to help you approach your days and your decisions from a spiritually guided place rather than a reactive state. Getting grounded is one of these things. Being grounded or centered brings you out of that reactive headspace, down to this amazing planet that we live on, and into a keen awareness of your body. It brings you out of the what-ifs and into the now, and it tells those impostor voices to shush.

Grab your journal. What are some activities you do when you need to unwind or de-stress? I don't mean just at the end of a workday, but how about when something is on your mind and you need to let it go? I used to go for a run to de-stress but found that it just worked my mind up even more, so now if I need to get grounded, I go for a long walk. Some people journal, some do deep breathing exercises.

Sometimes grounding habits can be as simple as getting outside. You can certainly have multiple habits that you turn to. These habits, if done in regular practice instead of just in reaction to rough feelings, can help keep you centered when you might otherwise let anxiety, fear, and impostor voices creep in. They're like a reset button. Give yourself permission to hit your reset button and to get familiar with the feeling of being reset, recentered, and grounded.

Even though meditation is growing in popularity for its numerous benefits, like reducing stress and anxiety, many people are intimidated by the idea of having to clear out all their thoughts. However, there are many kinds of meditation. Some focus on breath, others on clearing your mind, and some are visualizations.

Visualization is another simple tactic you can incorporate. This one is super powerful for me and makes it really easy to shift my energy and reset or recenter when my head gets carried away. Think about it: if you close your eyes and visualize yourself on the beach next to the calming sounds of the waves (or wherever your happy place is) and take some deep breaths with that image in mind, your heart rate decreases, your mind settles, and you just generally feel better!

There is one visualization that I started practicing

in traffic every morning (with my eyes open, of course). I would envision the huge light in the sky. (You know when you're on a plane flying above a thunderstorm and as far as you can see is sunshine reflecting off the tops of the clouds? That light.) Then I would picture it coming down and filling me up, starting with the top of my head. Every day that I did this, instead of getting to work frazzled and frustrated from sitting in traffic, I would arrive at peace and feeling more connected to God . . . and those days always went much smoother.

Meditation is the last grounding tool that I will mention here, and it is key to hearing your inner voice clearly, without the influence of impostors. There is a great comparison between meditation and prayer that really resonated with me the first time I heard it: Prayer is *talking* to God. Meditation is *listening* to God. It's easy if you grew up around religion to pray, pray, pray, but we have got to usher in the habit of stopping to listen . . . especially when we are in the midst of a life-altering decision.

Meditations don't have to be closed-eye moments of silence, either. You can most definitely use music (I like to put on headphones). Choose something that is not going to get your mind all fired up again. Choose an instrumental, beta waves, or even white noise (ocean sounds are some of my favorites).

The first time you meditate can be intimidating, but remember, all you have to do is *be*. Get in a comfortable position in a still and quiet place and just be.

You know who, I suspect, was really freaking good at meditation? David. It's all over the Psalms:

Psalm 37:7: "Be still before the Lord and wait patiently for him" (NIV).

Psalm 46:10: "Be still and know that I am God" (NIV).

Psalm 62:5: "My soul, wait silently for God alone" (NKJV).

Don't let meditation intimidate you. The connection to the Spirit that is fostered by meditation is so powerful. Let's go over some easy steps you can take to get acquainted with meditation.

STEP 1: GET COMFORTABLE

Lie face up on the ground, yoga mat, or comfortable cushion (not snooze-worthy comfortable, though). Wiggle your upper body so your shoulders are down away from your ears. Put your feet flat on the floor, rock your hips until your lower back is comfortable, and let your knees fall together so they are supporting each other.

STEP 2: BREATHE

Now take some deep breaths. Breathe in through the nose, letting your lower belly expand, and out through the mouth or the nose, whatever is comfortable for you. Continue these breaths, four counts in and four counts out. Focus on the breath. If you have trouble focusing, simply focus on each number as you count.

STEP 3: CHECK IN WITH YOUR BODY

Intuition is called a "gut feeling" for a reason, ya know? Scan your body for tension. Trauma and emotions are held in the body, so where there is tension, there might also be emotion tied to a story that you did not recognize or a relationship that you need to take down off the pedestal. Start at your toes and, in your mind's eye, work your way up the body. When you hit a place of tension or pain, ask, "God, what do you have for me here?" and listen. What comes to mind? (When you open your eyes, you're going to jot these in your journal, but don't do it yet. Stick with the process; that is not all that is there.) The answer you hear might be emotional or it might be physical. Trust the answer that comes to your mind.

Once you have your answer, you can release the tension. Turn it over to the Universe. Give it to God. I like to envision it being tossed out of my body and the void it left in my body being filled up with light. Don't be alarmed if the same tension continues to come up as you practice meditation throughout the week. Things that run deep take time to clear, but by recognizing the tension, acknowledging it, and letting it go, you are making progress.

STEP 4: CONNECT

After the body scan, take a few deep breaths. With each exhale, imagine sinking deeper into the ground. If you're feeling daring, you can envision sinking through each layer of dirt until you reach the core of the Earth. It should feel like a cocoon, a feeling of being supported and loved, knowing you are not alone. Ahh, that amazing creation, nature, and the connection to God that it brings forth when we take the time to be in awe of it. Take a few breaths to be thankful for that.

Now let's sit up. (Yes, you can open your eyes to sit up.) Get comfortable again in your seated position. Sometimes I sit cross-legged on a cushion on the floor. Sometimes I sit in a chair or on the sofa with some pillows behind me so that my feet touch the floor. Once you're comfortable, take a few deep breaths. When you're ready, on the exhale, I want you to imagine the space above the clouds where the most light is. (You remember.) Send your energy up there. Now we are going to scoop that light up and bring it down to fill up your body. Some people picture a laser beam. Some people picture liquid light. Whatever feels good to you is the right way. This is a great visualization that allows the high vibrational energy, or, if you will, the presence of God, to fill you up.

Visualize the light filling up your body. You can go from bottom to top like water filling up a glass. I like to imagine it coming through my crown and taking its time filling me up from the top down, washing away any negative energy that does not need to be there.

STEP 5: EXPAND

When the light has worked its way through your body and you're a vessel full of liquid light, on your next deep breath out (wait, you have been breathing this whole time, haven't you?), imagine the light inside you pushing outward on the edges of your skin. Then let it burst through and create a sphere around you. As you continue to breathe, let the sphere grow. Expand your light as far as you feel led to. You might even expand it past your city or even country. What does this have to do with connecting to Spirit? God is the light and will meet you right where you are. Now you are ready to be still and listen.

STEP 6: BE STILL AND KNOW

Now that your energy is expanded and you feel connected, just breathe and listen. It might be challenging not to have a conversation with God or your logic, and it's okay if a little of that comes up, but our primary objective at this moment is to listen. Focus on your breath, the light that is filling you up, and your gratitude for that.

STEP 7: TRUST

Trust the thoughts that come up. It wasn't until I really started trusting the whisper that I could hear it even more clearly and more often. The thoughts that come up objectively and independently are the ones you need to listen to. It's easy to let your logic question them: "Is this really Spirit-led guidance? Maybe I'm making this up?" I know the feeling. The thoughts that judge what comes up—or fire up the what-ifs—are impostors. The challenge is that we are so used to judging even our own thoughts through the filter of expectations and brules that when our inner voice speaks truth, we often toss all our junk on top of it and then we can't hear it anymore. This especially happens when it is telling us something that challenges an expectation or sparks a fear. We can logic that voice of truth right out of our heads.

There are additional steps that you can add on to make this experience even richer. You can learn to get answers through sensations that show up in your body. You can clear limiting beliefs and stories you've been telling yourself quickly by learning to let the Spirit work through your energy. You can learn more about embodiment and how to listen to your intuition through your body. Wherever you are right now is a great place to start. You have a wise, deeply rooted inner voice, and you will hear it—if you clear out all the baggage, listen, and trust.

In Luke 11:9, God promises, "Ask and it will be given to you; seek and you will find; knock and the door will be opened to you" (NIV).

When you're done listening (for this meditation, anyway), when you're ready, open your eyes and journal about whatever came up. You might even expand on it (still listening). What did you hear? And if you're not sure, what do you think you heard?

If you get these thoughts on paper, you can come back to them later. Don't be surprised if you read them weeks or even years from now and grin at how you can now recognize what you were so unsure was the Spirit's voice.

Making this a daily habit will not only help you hear Spirit's guidance in that moment, but you will also hear it more clearly as you navigate each day because you've checked in; you started your day with connection; you've gotten centered. The Spirit speaks through intuition. Trust what you are hearing now; you've heard it before. I know I'm not the only one who has prayed, "God, I'm running late, please show me where my keys are" and suddenly had the urge to look somewhere I hadn't looked before—or to look somewhere one more time—and there they were. You've taken the steps to quiet the impostors; if you stay on your guard so you can recognize them and kick them out when they try to intrude, you will be able to hear Spirit-led guidance through your intuition.

I don't expect you to do your first meditation and know what your answer is for your relationship, but if you make this a daily habit and consistently journal the messages you receive, you will be divinely guided. Do you see why it was so important to silence the impostor voices first? Can you imagine trying to listen to God with all of those outside voices in your head?

You will get your answer using these habits. Don't second-guess yourself. (I know, easier said than done!) Be diligent about journaling the thoughts that come up. Clarity will come.

Once you know what your decision is, processing it is a new battle. Revisit these exercises as often as you need. Even after your decision is made, you can continue to move forward by meditating, listening, and trusting what comes up.

This is worth saying again:

> *So I say to you: Ask, and it will be given to you; seek and you will find; knock and the door will be opened to you. For everyone who asks, receives; and the one who seeks, finds; and to the one who knocks, the door will be opened.*
>
> — LUKE 11:9–10 (NIV)

There is one *big* factor that we have not touched on yet: the kids.

If you have kids, if you don't have kids, if you want kids, or if you even just think you might have kids in the future, stick with me. I'm going to begin with a story for you.

During my first divorce, I was spilling my guts to my childhood best friend, Jennifer, at dinner one night. Was I doing the right thing? I had gone to couples' counseling with him. I was in counseling by myself. He wanted me to come back; should I do it? There were so many what-ifs swimming in my brain, and living up to everyone else's expectations (even though I may not have realized it) was not the least of them. Jennifer, who had heard all the horror stories as they happened (to this day, there are things that I don't remember that she will not tell me), looked me dead in the eye and said, "Ginny. What if you go back and he treats your kids the way he treats you?"

That was enough. I never looked back. I wasn't a mom yet, but I knew that I would be someday, and I couldn't bear the thought of my children being treated the way I had been by that man.

So, so, so many women have told me how they have stayed in terrible relationships for the sake of their children, and I cannot imagine how tough that must be. It's not that you should toss your relationship out to protect your children, but if you dig deeper, you will see what your children actually need protection from. Are you staying to protect them from feeling different from their friends whose parents are together? Are you staying so they won't be ridiculed at church? What are you protecting them from, Mama Bear?

Kids are little energy sponges. If you are trying to keep their lives as "normal and stable" as possible by staying but are arguing all the time or are unhappy, they will pick up on that, even if you think they don't notice. Even if they don't see what's going on with their eyes, they soak up your energy. What are they absorbing from you staying in this situation? Are they learning a lack of respect of boundaries? Are they learning that it is okay to let people treat you with disrespect?

Let's swing it the other direction too. If you leave, will they learn that when things get hard, the right thing to do is to walk away? I challenge you to examine your intentions when considering your kids.

Just like that inner voice of truth guides you in your decision through your intuition, it will guide you with your children, too. Whether or not you decide to reconcile your relationship, your kids have likely absorbed some trauma from what has happened thus far. (We all do. You can't protect them from all of life's trauma.) What are your kids picking up on in your relationship? How is it manifesting in their lives? Our kiddos are not developed enough to go through the steps of identifying brules and expectations or sometimes even identifying emotions; they just react.

Do a little digging around this and see what comes up. Writing down what you've noticed in your child is a good place to start, whether it's emotions, behaviors, or actions, positive or negative. Simply being aware rather than reacting (which is so easy to do, especially when you're in this sensitive place too) can open up a whole door of knowingness when it comes to your child.

If you've been practicing grounding habits and meditation, you might immediately feel that intuitive voice telling you how your child is being affected. Let it come up and trust it. If you don't hear it, don't worry; you have all the tools you need to feel it. Be persistent. (There's no doubt that a mother's intuition makes this whisper even louder, and I bet you trust it a whole lot more than the whispered answers you get for just yourself.)

Follow your meditation steps, but instead of focusing on what comes up for you, focus on what comes up about your child. Ask God. (There might be some related emotions that come up for you as well. Let yourself feel them.) Debunk the impostors by recognizing the comparisons and expectations that you have for your child. When you're ready to sit up and open your eyes, journal about what you heard.

Many intuition teachers, including the woman who first taught me how to develop my intuition, Dr. Haile Michaelson, teach about hearing the body tell you "yes" and "no" as you ask different questions. Haile is a retired naturopathic doctor and an expert in the body. Although she does not come from the same religious background that I do, I learned so much from her about how God created our bodies and how to be more aware of this earthly form we've been given.

God absolutely speaks through our bodies. Practicing listening to yes and no through your body requires you to really get in touch with all sensations in your body and to be acutely aware of what is going on inside. There is so much to teach around that that it merits its own book, but it is a skill that can really be helpful for fostering answers about your children, other people in your life, and yourself.

A former mentor of mine once put it this way: You have inner wisdom about what you need and what your children need, and the magic comes from asking God to help you create a path forward. Your best path may be true north and your kids' best path may be a little more east. So north-east will likely become the direction that feels right as you tune into your wisdom. You don't need to put your best path over your children's best path or theirs over yours, but instead ask for help and guidance to find the path that's right for both.

Now that you've identified how your children actually factor in, how to best connect with them and protect them, and how to ask for guidance on what is best for you and for them, we've got to address the impostors again. I am sorry to tell you that there is a whole crew of impostors totally dedicated to your identity as a mother. *Ouch.*

Set down the weight that you are carrying with these expectations of you as a mother. You have all the tools you need to debunk the expectations and brules in this area of your life. Take a moment or even a few days to sit with this, meditate, and ask yourself what exercises would be most beneficial for you to approach through the lens of motherhood. Is it identifying brules or limiting beliefs? Dropping expectations? Leveling the playing field so you can recognize your value among other moms?

Look at the exercises you just achieved in this chapter: tuning in to your children, learning to connect instead of react, choosing what is best for them and for you . . . all using your intuition. You are an amazing mother!

These beliefs we pick up about ourselves are storylines. As Brené Brown says, "The story I'm telling myself is . . ." Just because you tell yourself this story does not make it true.

My mother had so many storylines about being a mother. She believed that to be a good mom and a good Christian, she needed to stay home with us, which was just not financially possible. But as her child living through that experience, I learned that I can do it all. I can have a family and be a great mom *and* have a career that I love.

I can only imagine how easy it is to base your whole identity on motherhood. It is all around us (#momlife), but a mom is not all that you are. You are an amazing spirit who has been given a life and passions and experiences that are unique to you. You've been given this life not to suffer through, but to grow and learn. Just like we teach our children when they don't make the team or don't get the part they want in the play, it's not a reflection of their character. We encourage them to learn from the experience and use it to grow.

What may feel like a failure to you now is not really failure—it's an experience that is helping you become. Remember what Margery Williams said about becoming in *The Velveteen Rabbit?*

"You become. It takes a long time. That's why it doesn't happen often to people who break easily, or have sharp edges, or who have to be carefully kept. Generally, by the time you are Real, most of your hair has been loved off, and your eyes drop out and you get loose in the joints and very shabby. But these things don't matter at all, because once you are Real you can't be ugly, except to people who don't understand."

Be brave enough to become real, and your children will follow.

> *Start children off on the way they should go, and even when they are old, they will not turn from it.*
>
> — PROVERBS 22:6 (NIV)

Eight chapters is not enough time to make a wise decision. To really come to a Spirit-led conclusion, you need to give yourself time and space to wrestle with the inner work. Beliefs that you have held nearly all your life are not likely to dissolve overnight. In fact, there might even be something comforting about those old familiar beliefs. The natural end to that sentence would be "that have served you for so long"—but have they served you? Are they serving you now?

Stepping out into something new can be exciting, but it can also be so uncomfortable. There's comfort in going with the flow and not rocking the boat. Telling the impostor voices, "Yes, sir," and doing what they are telling you is comforting and yet creates such an uncomfortable life! I promise you that if you are diligent with the inner work, you will get a clear answer. You will feel good about your decision and confident in your path to get there.

What does a day in the life of a woman who is making a Spirit-led decision look like? Let's map it out. What does a normal day look like for you? Write it down (or pull out your handy planner). Where in this schedule can you fit in time dedicated to doing the inner work? Do you spend fifteen minutes in a quiet time with God each day? Can you turn that into twenty-five and add in even just ten minutes of meditation to listen, to see what comes up and begin to trust it? Do you spend thirty minutes (likely more, because, welcome to the era of binge-watching) in front of the TV at night? Can you take a walk alone instead?

Wrestling with the exercises in the previous chapters can be overwhelming, but it can be invigo-rating, too. Follow your intuition, noticing what comes up, and give yourself permission to tackle just that, only what comes up in the moment. Maybe it's deep-rooted beliefs or brules one day and expectations the next. Maybe it's enjoying dreaming and writing down the things you want in your life or your passions. Whatever it is, follow the thread for that day. You might need to spend more time on one thing in particular, and that is okay.

As you work the exercises into your daily routine, you'll notice when the impostor voices pop up during the day, and you'll be able to call them out—inevitably evoking a smile. Be proud of yourself as you start to notice them. This is how you begin to shift. The more you shift into alignment with your true self, the clearer everything will feel, and you'll trust those whispers of the Spirit more.

The hard part is staying in alignment when you just want to react. Even if you thought you let go of the ultimatums, when one is not met, you could easily find yourself thinking, *That's it. That is my sign. I'm done.* Slow down, sister. The times you feel like reacting are great times to go back to a grounding habit. Even if you can't leave the house or get away from the kids to go for a walk, can you take a few deep breaths? With each deep breath in and out, tap a finger on your right hand with your thumb— thumb to index finger, thumb to middle finger, thumb to ring finger, thumb to pinky. You've had four deep breaths to get grounded. The light visualization is another great one to do when you can't get away. Go up to the light, bring it down to earth, and fill yourself up with light. This practice not only has psychological effects but also physical ones, calming our nervous systems.

Your answer might get crystal clear shortly after you begin this work, or you might need more time. You might have more to work through or limiting beliefs that you are not yet ready to address. You don't have to level every playing field, clear all the unfounded beliefs, and call out all the brules before you come to a conclusion. But you do have to continue the work as you move forward. Impostor voices will sneak in, and staying in the habit of listening to your inner voice will help you stay clear as you move forward with your new life.

The emotions that come up will also try to sway you, grief especially. Grief doesn't just apply to death. You can feel grief for any loss, big or small, whether you are moving on with your life or just moving into a new house—it's okay to grieve that amazing closet space! Seriously though, your relationship hasn't been all bad or you would not have been with him in the first place. If you have decided to leave, you have to let yourself grieve the loss of the good. That is hard when you are trying to move on. Honestly, it's just easier to stay mad, and maybe that is what you need to push you forward. But promise me that, when you're in a safe place in life, you will grieve the good things, the things you loved, the happy memories.

On the other hand, if you are reconciling your relationship, you have likely decided to make some changes. Maybe you've had to let go of some expectations. Maybe you've had to let go of some comparisons. If you're competitive like me, you might easily get caught up in the comparison game. It can be hard to let go of climbing that ladder, all in the name of bettering yourself or your career. Coming home to yourself and what you really want can make the process of letting go of the things you don't want feel invigorating instead of like a struggle.

When Christie decided to leave her husband, she didn't grieve the end of the relationship with him. He was terrible to her. Mental, emotional, and verbal abuse was rampant in that relationship, and she had no regrets once she was able to make a clear decision that she felt confident in. What she did grieve was the loss of her relationship with his kids. She could have stayed in touch, but she didn't feel like it was safe for her—or healthy for either of them. So many tears were shed over the loss of those relationships. She didn't want the kids to feel like she abandoned them. She wanted them to know that she loved them. But she couldn't control any of that when she gave up the relationship with their father. (She wouldn't have been able to control their feelings even if she had stayed in touch, by the way.)

She literally gave her relationship with those kids to God. She prayed for them every day, and eventually she was able to move past the grief and appreciate everything she learned about herself during her time with them. Several years went by, and one of the kids reached out to her to say he missed her and loved her. She was pleasantly surprised and relieved to know that he knew she loved him. She would not have been able to come to that conclusion if she had not continued the inner work she started while making that decision and let herself feel all the emotions that came up as she powered through her course of action.

If you are not in a dangerous situation, give yourself the grace and the time to make a decision you feel confident in. Return to your grounding habits daily. Don't hesitate to ask yourself, "What is the most loving thing I can do for myself in this moment?" when things feel tough. Power through the inner work, as challenging as it is, and no matter how much it pushes you out of your comfort zone. If you make a quick decision when things get tough on your path forward, which they are bound to do, you will question your judgment and find yourself back at square one.

Now that you have quieted impostor voices, written down what you really want, and sorted through some feelings that come up, do you feel a clear knowingness of what you are supposed to do? That is your answer. Trust it. Do you only detect an inkling? Trust that too. Ask God, the Universe, or even your intuition what else there is for you to know. Pray for clarity and continue to listen with trust in yourself and the deep inner knowingness that is instilled in you.

I found myself questioning my answer so many times. *That can't be what God is telling me to do*, I thought, but when I shoved the brules aside, it *was* what God was telling me to do. How my life would be different if I had made a Spirit-led decision *before* I walked down the aisle! If I hadn't crowdsourced my confidence, if I hadn't listened to all of the voices telling me what my life was supposed to look like, what I should do, what success is. What if I had defined all of those things for myself first and made a decision based on who God made *me* to be? What if I had let intuition guide my steps instead of all of the "shoulds" that were constantly tossed my way?

You have your answer, and now you have to trust it. Just like Spirit gave you a clear answer, you'll also get a clear time and way to initiate whatever conversation needs to happen with your partner. The answer might be "just wait and let it reveal itself; it will be easier than you think," so fire up your patience if you need to. Follow the steps that you now know, and let the Spirit guide you. It might still be uncomfortable, but it will be clear.

Be courageous. You deserve it.

> *Trust in the Lord with all your heart, and lean not on your own understanding. In all your ways acknowledge him, and he shall direct your paths.*
>
> — PROVERBS 3:5–6 (NKJV)

Remaining stuck in indecision is really the only *easy* path here. We are going to discuss that in a later chapter, but for now, I want to discuss the decision you've made. If you chose to leave, it is hard. If you chose to stay, it is hard. Take a moment to acknowledge all the hard work you've done to get to the place where you are now. Though your conclusion might lead to a hard road ahead, and dread might be seeping in, do you feel confident that your decision was Spirit-guided, uninfluenced by the expectations of others?

I don't know about you, but my reaction is to depend on signs rather than trust my intuition. My inner dialogue sounds something like, "I think I'm supposed to ____, but if he does ____ (or reacts like ____), then that will be my sign that it's the wrong choice."

First, let me point out that there is nothing wrong with signs, unless they are overriding our intuition. Sometimes I look back at the decisions I've made in the past and have to send up a little prayer: "God, I'm so sorry I made you shout the answer at me when you were whispering to me all along."

There is also nothing wrong with choosing for the present. In my second marriage, I faced this decision over and over again (and that was before I had this method mapped out, although some of these tools were already present in my life). I prayed and prayed, "God, I know this does not feel right; I feel squashed; I feel suffocated, but I don't know what else to do," and several times the answer was, "Stay, love him to the best of your ability, and just keep praying." So that is exactly what I did, until the week that I now know was our last.

Things had gotten really bad, and I didn't know if staying or going was the right thing to do. My prayer at that time was, "God, if you want me to leave, you are going to have to make it impossible for me to stay," and two days later, I was violently kicked out of my own house and never looked back. (Not quite the "impossible" I was looking for, but it worked.) Sometimes you need the shove, but make sure that you are listening to the whisper. (The shove can be traumatizing and, trust me, it is not fun.)

The next step is to map out a plan. Do this intuitively as well. Follow the same steps you learned earlier for meditation and listen to the guidance you get. If you have chosen to stay, you'll want to make plans to mend the relationship and maybe even allow it to shift. Revisit the work you did in the first few chapters for this. Remember that you cannot base your path forward on your expectations of your spouse or the relationship; it has to be based on agreements. And you might even have to start with opening the conversation up to those agreements.

Finding a good relationship therapist or coach is a great first step. My advice here: be picky! You have got to use your intuition for this, too. Don't choose one that will take either side if you're going together. Maybe even choose to see one on your own for a while.

I've seen several therapists over the years, and they are each different. I had one who could always find a problem with me. She had me convinced that my concern about my boyfriend's strange behavior was an addiction to love—that I was the problem. A few months later, I found out that he was indeed cheating on me (the woman found my number and called me to throw it in my face), and I tossed that *Addiction to Love* book the therapist had given me right in the trash. Hopefully you find a therapist who is tapped in to intuition instead of brules. You might also explore the option of a relationship coach. The job of a coach is to ask powerful questions, listen, and reflect back to you, which is sometimes exactly what we need in order to see that we are living by expectations and brules. A coach will also help you identify the patterns that keep you stuck and teach you how to shift those patterns, if you're ready to.

Whether you have chosen to stay or to leave, you are going to need a support system. You cannot assume that your best friends or closest family members are going to be the safest place for you to run when you feel like falling apart. Blasting them with heavy topics and negative energy is the best way to push them away and remain isolated.

I am not saying you should not depend on your friends and family, or that you should suppress your emotions when you need to vent. What I am saying is that your first stop should be going inside yourself, touching base with your intuition and with God. You might discover that you are getting all worked up over thought patterns that don't belong there.

Once you've checked in with yourself, reach out to someone you trust, and before you start processing with them, ask if they have emotional bandwidth to talk about it. (Maybe not in those words if that is not really how you speak; we don't want them freaking out!) When we are in the middle of tough experiences in life, it is so easy to forget that other people have things going on too, but even our relationships with people in our support system are a two-way street.

The mindful tools you used in the first few chapters are still great for many types of decisions, but there are also tools you can use to help process your decision and all of the hard emotions that come along with it.

Journaling is great for this. Several emotions might surface. Start by writing down one of them, leaving some space to elaborate. Where is this emotion coming from? For example, if you are feeling anxious, is that anxiety based on fear? Fear of what? Is there an expectation or a storyline causing that fear?

Storylines are beliefs we adopt that set up the expectations we have for ourselves. Most of the time, they are based on experiences that we've had. For example, my experience participating in fitness competitions created the storyline that I am not desirable unless I'm in competition shape. That word "desirable" held multiple stories/beliefs for me. For one, I believed that I was not attractive unless I was in competition shape, and secondly, I believed that my personal training services would not be in demand unless I was in competition shape. Can you see how, with this storyline, I began placing my value in my looks?

Let's keep rolling with this example. During a breakup, I was once told, "You're never going to find someone who is okay with you gaining the extra five pounds you gained when you dated me." First of all, let's go ahead and hike that giant red flag up the flagpole. Secondly, had I not already done the work on that belief, his comment totally would have factored in to my decision to stay or to go in that relationship.

Based on this example, this exercise would look something like this:

Emotion: Anxiety (or guilt or shame—this storyline brings up a bunch!)

This emotion is based on: The fear that I won't find anyone else.

Storyline: I'm not attractive the way that I am now.

I challenge you to dig deep into those storylines

and journal about when you think they were first created. If you are having trouble remembering where the story started, ask during one of your meditations. Your subconscious already knows. Identifying these storylines helps us see them for what they are and helps us change our related thought patterns. If we can easily recognize those thoughts when we have them throughout the day, we can more easily kick out those impostor voices and hear the truth about ourselves.

No matter your choice, I can guarantee you will feel grief at some point. Grief comes from any sort of loss. Let me say that again: *any* sort of loss. Remember all those expectations you had of your relationship? You might even remember the life you envisioned or hoped for as you entered the relationship or even as you walked down the aisle. Those are losses, and they deserve to be grieved. If you've decided to stay, your relationship still might be different than you imagined, and you might have chosen to give up some of your expectations in exchange for some agreements with your partner. You need to grieve the things that you have lost, even if they are dreams and expectations.

Sometimes these losses are hard to recognize because we are busy comparing our experience to everyone else's. As I mentioned earlier, in my mid-thirties, I went through IVF and transferred an embryo that didn't stick. When I found out, I shut down. I didn't talk to anyone for two weeks, not even my best friend whom I usually talked to every day. I went to work (where I could pretend that hard experience didn't exist), and when I went home, I headed straight to bed. I struggled to figure out why I couldn't snap out of my funk, until one day I realized that it was a loss. Not everyone agreed with my decision to choose IVF, including some important people in my life, and so many people I knew had experienced actual miscarriages. I was not even acknowledging my loss because it was technically not a miscarriage; the story I was telling myself was that it didn't count. Once I acknowledged my loss and let myself feel all the emotions that came with it, I was able to move forward and ease out of my funk.

Some of the best advice I've ever been given is from one of my therapists (in fact, the only one I keep in touch with). She has always confronted me with just the right combination of compassion and bluntness. The summer that I experienced multiple major losses, she told me, "The only way you are going to get to the other side of this is to go through it. You have to let yourself feel these emotions." I can still hear her voice saying this to this day.

While every fear has a storyline, every emotion does not. Do not explain your emotions away. Acknowledge them. Feel them. And release them. This is true even for emotions that are attached to storylines—you still must acknowledge them; be grateful that you can recognize and feel the emotion; and then let it go.

While you move to your next chapter in life, whether it is reconciliation or separation, you will have many losses to grieve. Even in this part of the process, it's important to drop those comparisons.

During the summer that I lost my mom while going through a second divorce, I picked up a flyer off a table at the women's center where I was doing an intake for domestic violence counseling.

The flyer was for a group called the Grief Recovery Method. I knew I was grieving, I just didn't know quite the depth of all the things I was grieving that summer. At our first group, we went around the circle and talked about our losses; I went last. As my story of fearing for my life, not having anywhere to live, and then burying my mother in the midst of it all unfolded, I could see the other ladies' jaws creep closer and closer to the floor. I told the whole story with hardly a tear, stunned at the shock of what my life had become. But I took to heart what the leader stated before we all shared:

"No one's loss is greater than another's. Grief of your loss runs just as deep."

So, whether you are grieving the life you dreamed of, not being home with your kids, lost years in a relationship that didn't work, or your dream house, it is a loss, and you have the right to grieve. Let yourself feel all the feels, and let meditation and those grounding habits help you. Remember, the body holds emotions, so being connected to your body during this time is especially important for letting your emotions pass through.

During Katie's breakup, she found herself breaking out in a rash on her arms, legs, and chest. It took a few tries, but as she meditated daily and asked God what was causing the reaction, the word "stress" kept coming up. She didn't trust it at first. Of course she was stressed, but how could she escape it?

While she couldn't escape the stress, she could do things to counteract it. She started going to yoga and gave herself permission to not talk to anyone. (Tough for an extrovert to not make new friends, but she needed that sacred time and space for herself.) She noticed her stress level dropping, and the rash was soon gone.

The simplest moments can trigger emotions, and you have to give yourself enough grace to let them come up. I remember being upstairs at my parents' house the day of my mom's funeral, slipping on my black dress. (I know it's acceptable to not wear black to funerals, but in my heart there was no other option; my whole life just felt dark.) I got the zipper up as far as my shoulder blades. Normally, I would ask my mom or my husband to help me get it the rest of the way to the top, but neither was there. It was one of the loneliest moments of my life.

Months later, my dad posted something on my Facebook page (or wall, or whatever we're calling it now). It said something like, "Someday, someone will come along and hug you so tight that all your pieces stick back together." A well-meaning friend commented, "Jesus is the only one who can put your pieces back together." (Can I get ~~an Amen~~ a go screw yourself?) So often, when people don't know what to say or what to do, they just toss you a Band-Aid. Yes, God is a God of redemption, the God who heals, but I did not need a Jesus Band-Aid, I needed a f*ing hug.

God has put the power we need to heal within us, and if you keep going within and seeking Spirit-led guidance, you'll find yourself surrounded with the support you need at exactly the right time. Let your needs come to the surface. Show yourself some love and grace. Let people help you. Let people love you. And continue to go within for your answers.

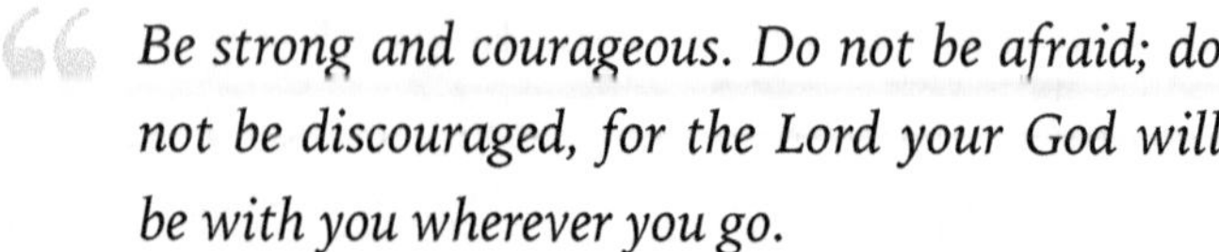

Be strong and courageous. Do not be afraid; do not be discouraged, for the Lord your God will be with you wherever you go.

— JOSHUA 1:9 (NIV)

Whether you stay or you go, there is one thing that remains true: you have to be the one to take care of you. Of course, you should let people help you when you need it. It's important to surround yourself with support. At this point in your journey, you have either decided to leave or you have decided to stay and have probably realized that you need to set some agreements with your partner.

Research shows that it's very likely that some of those agreements involve you being taken care of. Listen, if he hasn't been willing or able to uphold those agreements thus far, you can't expect him to uphold them now. If reconciling your relationship is the Spirit-led conclusion you have come to, you are going to have to drop the expectations. You can still be provided for in this relationship, but your expectations might need a realistic reboot. In a similar light, if you have chosen to end your relationship, you might be wondering how you will provide for yourself financially.

We could poll one hundred different women, all with different circumstances and who have come to different conclusions, and finances will still be an area that needs to be empowered in nearly every woman. Let me tell you, when you realize this is something you can give yourself, you will be unstoppable.

During my second marriage, I had handed over the reins financially, not because I wanted to but because I was forced to. So, during our divorce, I found myself relieved that I would no longer have someone sucking my bank account dry. However, I had also taken a more than 50 percent pay cut to take a job that was better for my family, so it was still a bit scary.

There are so many amazing financial resources that have changed my life, and I know they will change yours. I'm going to go in order here:

1. IF YOU CHOOSE TO EARN MORE INCOME, DO SOMETHING YOU LOVE THAT LOVES YOU BACK!

I stayed at that job several months after my divorce, but it became more and more apparent that it was keeping me small. I put my feelers out and moved on to the next thing. I knew my strengths, I knew what I loved, I knew what I wanted to do every day, and I set out to find it. Boom: pay bump. When the next job no longer served me, I did it again, again highlighting my strengths and the new skills I had. Boom: another pay bump. Before I knew it, my income was back where I'd left off—and within the next four years, I had doubled it again (quadrupled from the pay cut job). Job-hopping is often frowned upon, and I'm not saying it's the best thing to do, but the brules apply here too! I found my strengths and my passions, and I always kept an eye on what was going on in my field—what companies were looking for and what skills I wanted to gain in a certain position.

Erica chose to stay in her relationship, but she decided to start bringing in her own income to give herself more financial freedom. She knew that keeping an organized schedule was one of her strengths and something she enjoyed. She followed her intuition and started a business helping other women create systems for getting and staying organized. She also shifted her expectation that her partner would completely provide for her financially. The combination of the two (and a lot of inner work) revived their relationship.

You have probably already been bombarded with "side hustle" opportunities. Side hustles are a great way to go *if* you are doing them for the right reasons. So many multi-level marketing representatives recruit by promising extra money and "work from anywhere" opportunities. Those companies might be a great fit for you, but be picky. Break out that list of activities that light you up. Does your side hustle incorporate these? Could you start your own business incorporating them?

No matter what you choose, you have to take into account how much time and money it actually takes you to get off the ground. Make sure it is something that is aligned with who you are and what you love.

Guess what? You can use your Spirit-led decision-making skills to make business decisions too. You've heard the saying, "If you love what you do, you will never work a day in your life," right?

2. KNOW HOW TO MANAGE YOUR MONEY—AND BALANCE.

I'm not a crazy spender, but I admittedly am not the best at managing money or finding balance. If anything, I err on the side of the guilty spend. In my mid-twenties, I came across David Bach's book *Smart Women Finish Rich*, and it changed my life. Among several skills David teaches, there was an exercise in the book that had me write out goals—dreams, not just savings goals. If I wanted a new car, I wrote it down. If I wanted to go to Greece, I wrote it down. What?! This gave me permission to save for what I wanted, not what society or my grandparents told me I needed to have. (They *would* have told me to go to Greece, by the way.)

Over the years, as my income has increased, I've been very mindful of watching my spending and keeping a good balance between what I want and what I am totally content with. *And* I choose to delegate my weaknesses. I have no idea about investments, and it's not something that gets my blood pumping to learn. So, I hunted down a financial adviser to do it for me. You can use your Spirit-led decision-making skills to identify your weaknesses and find the right person to delegate to. I had (and probably still have) some serious brules to break around retirement savings. I feel obligated to invest anything I save, but my investment coach works with me on my goals—and not all of them are decades down the road. They are things I want to do now.

If you are reconciling and have joint finances, you might be thinking that this doesn't apply. Oh, but it does. If being taken care of financially is something that you want, there is an agreement to be made here, and it might involve you being able to find a way to make your own money.

3. GET YOUR MIND ON BOARD.

A few years ago, I picked up a book called *The Dynamic Laws of Prosperity* by Catherine Ponder, and I started reading four to five pages each day. Since then, my life has never been the same. The teachings in this book addressed some of the brules that I had been living by without even realizing it. As soon as I recognized them, I was able to change my mindset around money, and now it literally just shows up for me.

One thing that I was taught in my Christian upbringing that rings true is that money belongs to God. This belief made me feel like money was not mine to be had. Here's the thing. (Are you ready for some cold, hard truth?) Why would God not want to bless you with money?

There is a whole lot more to moving forward than just finances. No matter which path you've chosen, it's important to remember to take care of yourself. After finances, there are three more big considerations that can easily sneak up on you.

1. SHOW YOURSELF SOME LOVE.

Not unrelated to finances is self-care. Sure, you should indulge in that hobby, you should go on that trip, but listen: especially if you are responsible for yourself, part of self-care is making sure you are not in financial stress later. Love yourself enough to know when something is really benefiting you and when it is just an escape from reality.

We are going to take a deep dive into definitions here and look at self-care versus self-compassion.

There are so many women out there who get their nails and hair done and label that self-care. And maybe those things are self-care for you. Maybe those are relaxing moments that allow you to unwind and love your body. For me, those things are not self-care. Getting my hair and nails done is something I do because I want to, but that's not my relaxing time. Usually, I've squeezed my appointments between other things on my calendar and I'm multitasking from my phone with whichever hand is available. That is not self-care, *but* for me, saying "no" to something else so that I can take a long walk and listen to a book is self-care. That is how I unwind and reset. That is what makes me feel grounded. Your grounding habits are great places to start with self-care, and they are full of self-compassion too!

Self-compassion is loving yourself past the guilt, brules, expectations, and obligations. As you practice these habits and Spirit-led decision steps, you'll notice that your intuition gets clearer and clearer. If you feel that saying "yes" to something will bring stress or anxiety or will just give you lack of space, you will learn to accept that it's okay to say no!

I am an extrovert and a people-pleaser (gulp), so it is a constant battle for me to say no when I feel like I should say yes. Sometimes it's even hard for me to notice when I'm doing it. But choosing *you* is self-compassion—and you deserve that.

2. EMBRACE BOUNDARIES.

As you move into a new chapter in your life, you have to create boundaries, and I'm not just talking about saying no to obligations. Just because you've identified and worked through brules and expectations doesn't mean that people are going to stop flinging them at you. You have to do what you can to protect your energy. Sometimes this means backing off on time spent with someone who brings your energy, emotions, and mindset down. Sometimes it means creating an energy shield. Remember in meditation when you moved your light beyond your skin and expanded that energy in a growing bubble around you? Your brain does not know the difference between a visualization and reality. (There really is so much research on that!) So, if you know you're walking into a situation that could bring you down and you can't opt out, take some time to get into that bubble of protective light first—and don't let anyone burst it!

3. FIND YOUR TRIBE.

Picking up new hobbies, fostering the growing interests you have, and learning new things is a great way to find your tribe, the group of women whose energy is aligned with yours. If you are feeling judged at Bible study, it's not the place to find support. You don't have to give it up, but you can find another church to visit or a new group that is more accepting of where you are—take a break for a while. That is okay!

Take the time to nurture other interests, those passions that you've been neglecting or the things you put inside the circle of what you want in your life. You might find that, in that painting class you've been meaning to take, you find the support and encouragement you need. There's a strong belief among my family members that you have to have a church "home"—you have to be involved or you won't really have community. Quality connections can be found anywhere, often in the place you least expect. Find your tribe.

As you seek out things that light you up (see the list of things you lose track of time doing), you will see God bring people into your life who encourage and support you. The passions, gifts, and interests that you've been given are gifts to the world, and you bring yourself closer to your truest self by doing them. That is why they feel good!

If you're reconciling, carving out time for more of what you love might feel like a risky topic or might require an agreement to be made. If you're heading out on your own, finding time for these things might feel overwhelming, especially if you will be juggling kids too. But including time for the things you love in your life is such an important part of living a fulfilling life. Don't wait. Even if it's not as frequently as you would like, make it happen. I have no doubt that you will find a feeling of fulfillment and happiness beginning to creep in. Why? Because you are giving yourself permission to be you and feeding your soul with things that you love, things that God created you to do.

It is easy to fling yourself face-first into a new set of obligations masked as things that you love. Use the tools you've learned to decide what is fitting for you.

12

THE POWER OF
OWNING YOUR STORY

At this point, you are probably pretty clear on your decision. Because of my own experience, I have few examples to use relating to those who choose to stay, but I certainly don't want you to walk away feeling like if you've chosen to stay, you don't have a story to tell. You absolutely do.

There is a church in Houston that I used to attend frequently. The pastor and his wife have the most beautiful story of how God redeemed their marriage after they were separated for years. Maybe the heart of your story is not about your relationship. Maybe it is about how you kicked your people-pleasing habit or how you learned to hear the voice of the Spirit clearly by using your intuition.

What my life has proven true is that God is the Redeemer, and even if your relationship is not redeemable, your story certainly is, no matter how far gone you think it is.

I struggled for a long time, mostly during my second divorce, with the thought that I would be labeled "the girl who has been married twice." I even felt obligated to disclose that information quickly once I started dating again, like, "You better know what you're signing up for. Most people think I'm a walking disaster." The shame around divorce (or *divorces*, in my case) runs rampant in the Christian community. During my first divorce, other women even called my mother to tell her that *she* was a bad Christian for letting me get divorced and that the right thing to do would be to talk me into staying (staying with a man who quoted scripture while he took advantage of me; no thanks). So, I had a whole cheering section when I started crafting the mental storyline that I was ruined, tainted, and would never be good enough for anyone else.

In fact, I still battle the storyline that I am unworthy of pure love. I've embraced it with my head, but embracing it with my heart and soul, to the deepest core of my being, is a different level and will long be a work in progress.

It took me years to drop the idea that being

divorced twice was part of my identity. Slowly but surely, as the subject would come up, friends would say, "Oh yeah, I forgot about that!" After several of those moments, I realized that if my friends don't view me that way, I shouldn't view myself that way either! That is not to say that there isn't the occasional guy who, in the middle of an argument or breakup, will throw it in my face, but I know better —and that is a telltale sign that that guy is not for me.

I hope that the earlier chapters made you aware of the storylines that already exist for you. I want to challenge you, as you move forward, to be carefully aware of the storylines that you are creating for yourself. What is the story you're telling yourself? I hope it is that you are loved, you are supported, and you are worthy.

Remember back in chapter 2, when I was volun-told to tell my story at Bible study—and then volun-told by a (very loud) God-whisper to make my story of the two divorces? As my story unfolded that night at a table of strangers, most of them new to the church, I saw the girl across the table start wiping her eyes . . . then, waterworks. The next day, she emailed me, asking for her last name to be changed on the roster. We ended up meeting for a walk in the park. As it turns out, she too was in the process of leaving an abusive marriage, but she had not filed for divorce yet because, well, it would be her second one.

Vulnerably sharing something that is hard to talk about, or that is embarrassing, or that doesn't seem that important to you, creates a powerful connection, and all of a sudden, we are not alone. All of a sudden, we are in this together. (And you never know—out of that vulnerable moment, you might gain an invaluable relationship. That woman at the table and I have now celebrated years of friendship.)

As we become aware of storylines, we also have to be aware of new comparisons that sneak in. We are not comparing battle wounds. If you catch yourself thinking, *Wow, I don't have it that bad,* or, *She can't understand, my situation is way worse than hers,* kick that thought to the curb right now. The way to empower each other is to meet each other where we are with love and compassion.

There is a big difference between sharing your story because you know it can help other people and really truly owning your story. Owning your story does not happen overnight. Owning your story involves being proud of your story. How on earth can you be proud of something that carries so much shame? No matter what conclusion you have come to, it's highly likely that you feel like you've failed.

Whether you are fighting for a relationship that is failing or you have chosen to leave, it's embarrassing to admit defeat! The first step to owning your story is to simply be open to it. You are in the middle of the plot right now and you can't see where it is going. Just know that it is going somewhere good.

That moment on the floor of my empty apartment—when I decided that I didn't know why this was my story but I was going to own it—was the moment my life began to change. Instead of fighting to defend my past, I chose to let where I found myself in the present change me, giving my future meaning and purpose so that I could move forward and be better for it. I was open to letting the Universe use my experience not just to help others but also to foster my own growth, even if I didn't know what that would look like. It was a moment of tremendous faith. Hebrews 11:1 has always been one of my favorite verses, and looking back in that moment, it became real to me: "Now faith is confidence in what we hope for and assurance what we do not see" (NIV).

As you remain open and let yourself transform through your experience, you will begin to notice that your story was meant just for you. There is no one else on this planet who could live your story the way you are living it. There is no one more capable of conquering these challenges. At times, you might feel like this experience is going to kill you, but you've been entrusted with this situation because you and only you can let it evolve into something beautiful.

You heard part of my story earlier about telling my grandfather about my IVF journey. This, too, is part of my story. I've never been the woman who is married to the idea of having kids and a family, but as I got older and the opportunity arose, I knew it was something I wanted. So, I got involved with the Single Mothers by Choice community and chose to pursue that path. So many (y'all, so, so many) well-meaning family members and friends have said, "Oh, I just wish you were doing this with someone," their comments laced with pity.

Well, I don't! Sure, creating a family alone was not plan A, but I don't feel like it's plan B—it's just plan *me*. Do you know how hard this process is? It is *so* hard! Not just on my body, but also in terms of all of the decisions I have to make along the way: timing, donors, various testing, etc. This is not a path for just anyone, and I am proud of myself and the strength and the courage that it has taken me to choose it.

What virtues is your path in life bringing to light for you? These things make you uniquely you. They foster transformation, if you let them, and that is always something to be proud of.

Encouraging women to share their stories is a huge part of my mission in life, not just because of my own experience (although that does hold a lot of water), but because other people's stories have inspired and empowered me.

Through years of creating content, I've had the privilege of interviewing some of the most interesting people, and I've found that asking the right questions is key. I think I've made some enemies in the PR world because I never send a list of questions when they ask for them. I always respond, "My interviews are more like a conversation," which is not the answer they want to hear. I've found, though, that in these conversations, you often find a story that is less frequently heard but oh so powerful. So many of those little stories are worth telling! The interviews I've done have inspired me to take action in my life, like joining a Rodeo committee (a huge nonprofit in Houston), signing up for a painting class, and being "louder" about being myself!

No matter how insignificant you think a piece of your story is, if you are feeling led to share it, there is a life that needs to be touched by it. You have permission to be proud of your strength, of the life and challenges that God has entrusted you with, and of your journey through them, no matter how messy it may seem.

Are you missing all the journaling yet? Here's a good question to start with: What parts of your story do you think could empower and inspire others?

You have made it this far, through each of the steps, to get clear and come to a conclusion that you know is guided. You are probably going to talk it out with your friends, and that is okay. (I would too.) Just keep your guard up for the impostor voices. Be aware when you are seeking validation from sources outside of your inner voice and the deep wisdom that lives in you.

I'm going to tell you something that is going to be hard to hear. Ready? Indecision keeps you stuck. You can hash out all the pros and cons. You can revisit the steps in this book over and over again. But if you keep yourself in indecision-mode, you will never move forward. You'll be stuck. Stuck in this painful place that keeps you frustrated and keeps you small.

When I set out to write this book, it was not going to be about Spirit-led decision-making at all. It was going to be about how important it is to tell your story and how telling your story can help you heal. After much prayer and meditation, God (via my shouting inner voice) said, "Nope, you're going to write this instead."

"Okay, cool. I can do that, but my identity is storytelling. I've made my career in storytelling. It's the thing that I know the most about and that I'm known for. So how about both?"

"Nope." (Have you ever had those conversations with God?)

This was an ongoing argument for weeks on end, an internal battle, an earth-to-heaven dialogue that would not ease up. You can see who won that one.

I was on a walk one day, fully engaged in this back-and-forth conversation. (My neighbors probably think I'm crazy, because I'm not entirely certain it was all in my head.) Then, like a ton of bricks, it hit me: "This debate is keeping you stuck. It's the same situation I'm telling you to help women out of—indecision, the 'both,' or the 'I'll decide later.'" It was time to surrender. It was time to say, "Okay, God.

This is not what I had in mind, but I know there's a greater plan here."

"Let your yes be yes and your no be no," Matthew 5:37 (NKJV) says. If you've decided to stay and shift your relationship and the decision comes up again, you can decide again. However, if you have chosen to stay, you must take action to move forward. (In other words, you can't revisit the decision again tomorrow, or even next month!) Your choice to stay cannot be based on "if he . . ." or any expectations you have. You must drop your expectations and move forward with agreements. It might be helpful to revisit that chapter as you create your plan to move forward. Yep, making an agreement takes two parties, and your partner should also be willing to create agreements with you—and you've got to drop the expectation of what that looks like or what he's willing to agree to. Go in with a blank slate and be open to the information and inner guidance you get along the way without ultimatums.

If you suspect in the least that you are in an abusive relationship, please pick up a copy of *The Verbally Abusive Relationship* by Patricia Evans or visit PatriciaEvans.com for resources. Her book saved my life. I had no idea that verbal abuse was a thing (because God-fearing men don't abuse their wives, as I had been taught). Although I didn't leave that marriage until abuse was undeniable, her book introduced me to the cycle of abuse and made me aware of what was going on, which saved me from gaslighting and crazy-making, and ultimately set me free.

The inner work you've done and the habits you've developed will keep you grounded and your spiritual ears open. There will for sure be moments when you question your decision. When you feel yourself on shaky ground, go back to your grounding habits, the activities that make you feel better—a quiet walk, meditation, a long bath, whatever they are for you. Quiet your mind so you can listen to your heart and let yourself feel all the feelings that come up.

Identify the feelings and ease your way up the vibrational scale. You don't have to jump to something extreme, just choose one thought that feels better. That sounds easy, but I know that in the moment it might not feel easy, so let me give you an example. If you're thinking, *What if I've made the wrong decision?* you can choose to shift to *I made a guided decision and am supported.*

Your own thoughts are your biggest obstacle to moving forward, but you learned at the beginning how to break them down. I do a ton of thought work with my coaching and hypnotherapy clients. Everything begins in the mind. If you can create an aware-ness of your thoughts, you're on the path to victory over them. Notice in the example above, we did not take a negative thought and flip it to a glittery, overly positive thought. You have to believe the thought that you are turning to in order for it to shift your energy and your mindset. If we took *What if I've made the wrong decision?* and instead turned to *Everything is going to be fine*, that might be a lot harder to believe. But turning to *I made a guided decision and am supported* is more effective because it's a thought you know to be true, and it therefore has the power to shift you. You are learning to trust your own beautiful, powerful wisdom, and you can remind yourself anytime that you are doing the best you can, one step at a time.

Our thoughts evoke feelings, so if you struggle with identifying the thought, go to the feeling first. The best way? You guessed it: meditation. It's impor-tant, although not always comfortable, to quiet your mind and let your feelings come up. Some of us are exceptionally talented at stuffing our feelings, which makes it harder to let those feelings come up. Instead of sitting with them, we choose other thoughts, usually thoughts that keep our minds busy. Sitting with our feelings can be so uncomfort-able! It's a natural reaction to let your mind go to something else, but remember, the only way to move forward is to go through it. (Even once you master quieting your mind, it's tempting to try to race up the vibrational scale with positive thoughts that don't feel realistic. I challenge you to sit in the discomfort of the feeling, let it come up, wait for it, and have compassion for yourself.)

Go back to the meditation steps in chapter 6, and when you get to checking in with your body, ask yourself what is there. (You might actually be feeling it in your body—maybe a heavy chest, tension between your shoulder blades, pain lurking some-where.) Follow the thread: What thought comes to mind when you go to that area of discomfort? Your feelings might not be so buried that you have to identify a place in your body. They might surface easily. Let them.

Once you've identified a feeling, sit with it for a while, and let it exist without burying it, ask yourself what thought is evoking that feeling. (This will lead us to the next step of this exercise.) You might be surprised at what you find. Thoughts that often come up include fear: fear of letting other people down, fear of being alone, fear of never having the happy life you imagined. You might notice some impostor thoughts that surface: thoughts that are connected to expectations and comparisons. We know how to debunk those, but this time I want you to sit with the feeling and follow the thread. Go through the process while you are still quiet and connected. What belief is causing that expectation?

Identify the feeling and let yourself really feel it.

Ask yourself what thought is triggering that feeling.

What is the foundation of the thought? An outside source? An experience where you picked up a belief about yourself?

What is the belief about yourself?

What is actually true?

I want to give you an example. During a breakup, I received a lovely email from this scorned lover, stating what a terrible and unstable person he believed me to be. The email strongly resembled others from an abusive ex-husband, so this actually only confirmed to me that I had made the right decision by breaking up with him. Nevertheless, the initial sting of someone's words can be bothersome.

I forwarded the email to my brother, and his reply to me was the best gift anyone could have given me in that moment. His words: "Let me respond to this with truth." For each poisonous sentence in the original email, my brother had responded with a sentence of truth. For example, when the original email tied having multiple marriages to my character, my brother's replacement was that I did the best I could with the information I had at the time. (One realistic thought that feels better moves you up the vibrational scale.) The emotion that came up with that original email was unworthiness (which was exactly the sender's purpose, to make me feel unworthy). The thought? Well, there are so many—and so many lies. (If thoughts come up in a flood, it's okay to have a laundry list.) Make your list and leave room below each thought to respond with one that you know is true.

Recently, I came across a recording of my mom giving her testimony to a large group of women at Bible study. (I know I was a junior in high school at the time because she referenced one of my teachers, who was in the audience.) The recording (originally on a cassette) is about twenty minutes long and, although the message is positive, I can hear the beliefs she held about herself seeping through. I certainly heard some that carried over to me. Maybe some of these things are beliefs you hold too:

- My housekeeping isn't good enough because I have to work full time, and we also can't afford to hire someone to help. I have to do it all.

- To be a good Christian, I need to be at church every time the door is open.
- Although I love and enjoy praying, it is not important enough to keep up with all the stay-at-home moms who go to Bible study during the day.
- I was born with the feeling that I was destined to disappoint people, a fear of failure. Even that fear is a sin and disappoints God.
- Just being myself isn't good enough, and when I choose situations that allow me to be myself, other areas of my life will fail.
- Defining success is not my job; living up to it is. I have to measure up to everyone else's standards in order to be successful.
- I am not a good mom or a good Christian unless I stay home with my kids.
- I am not allowed to "just want to" stay home with my kids. Everything I want in life has to have a religious, financial, or familial justification. I am not worthy of living a life that I love just because I want to.
- I am alone because I am different.
- Disease is the only thing that is not my fault. I should be able to control

everything else, and even my health is something I control as much as possible.

It is so important that you leave space below each belief you write so you can respond to it with truth—and if you don't know what that truth is yet, that is okay. Just leave it blank. The truth is there and will come to you.

We are not going to solve all the root problems here (yet); that is a lifelong process of learning, knowing, growing, and learning, knowing, growing again. Right now, we are just overcoming the current obstacles. You made a guided decision, but sometimes the fear and the discomfort that come with that decision will bring you back to ground zero. This is why we did all those journal exercises. Revisit them. Some you may need to do again. But above all, check in with yourself, and be still and listen and know.

I wrote this book because if I'd had a crystal-clear method like this to make truly Spirit-led decisions, it would have saved me a lot of heartache, stress, and loss. I look back at decisions I made not just about my marriages, but about purchasing houses, making career moves, even committing to social activities, and can see my motivation was to please everyone else—everyone but me. In so many decisions, I kept myself boxed in by a false set of standards and "shoulds." I may have been at church every time the doors were open, but I was living out of alignment with the Spirit and the truest version of myself.

While I know that my decisions resulted in a rocky but beautiful collection of stories, I also know that sharing those stories can empower you to recognize, trust, and follow your intuition. My (sometimes uncomfortable) vulnerability could possibly change your life and save you heartache and stress—and a hell of a lot of inner conflict! If I can spare you any amount of pain and help you wrestle through your decision with grace, my goal will be accomplished.

The steps of Spirit-led decision-making can be broken down, and with practice (and simple awareness), you can use them for any decisions, big or small.

At this point, you should be able to recognize expectations, whether they are your own, those of society, or those that someone else has placed on you. Simply being aware of them is a huge step. While pulling out your journal and doing the exercises is a great way to really dig in, you can call out expectations as you notice them throughout the day. When you see these impostors for what they are, it is so much easier to kick them to the curb and prevent them from influencing your decision.

You have all the tools to drop your people-pleasing habit and feel confident being *you*. You can level the playing field, seeing qualities that you idolize about someone else in yourself too. You can bring the people you aim to impress or please to the same level that you are on. As you do this, you will find your fear of failure shrinking and your confidence increasing.

With the impostor voices quieted, you are able to listen to what is really in your heart, your deepest desires—what *you* want rather than what everyone else has, what others want for you, or what you "should" do. In the quiet, the Spirit meets us. We have to clear through the junk we've picked up along the way, but God speaks through our passions and desires.

Through daily meditation, you tap into your intuition. Prayer is the act of asking. Meditation is the act of listening. The Spirit speaks to us through our gut instincts, a deep knowingness, and even through our bodies. The more you make listening a habit, the clearer the voice of the Spirit will be. You'll recognize it more easily, trust yourself more, and become clear and confident in your decisions.

Remember how Matthew 5:37 told us to let yes be yes and no be no? Indecision keeps you stuck. So, once you hear that clear, small voice telling you the way to go, it's time to move forward. You will feel the flood of emotions either way, and the only way to get to the other side is to let yourself go through them. Let your emotions be used to wash away whatever is no longer serving you.

Call in the reinforcements. Show yourself compassion by not powering through something so hard alone. Care for yourself by allowing yourself to participate in activities that light you up. Hire a therapist to walk you through the tough patches or a coach to help reflect back to you things you might not see and to help you keep moving forward. Your tribe will rise up around you when you have made a Spirit-led decision. I've watched it happen so many times in my own life and in others' lives.

Own your story. Turn the page. Your story is not over. You have what you need to begin creating a life that you love. Be proud of it. I know it didn't turn out the way you planned (if it had, you wouldn't be reading this book). Mine didn't either, but I owned my story. I let it transform me. I chose to grow instead of staying stuck in an identity that wasn't meant for me. Now my life is beyond what I ever would have written for myself.

Give yourself credit for how far you have come! The steps in this book are not easy. You have bravely tackled some deep inner work. If you made it this far, that means you didn't give up when it got hard. I am proud of you!

I know I've given you a lot to practice daily, but if you can carve out two more minutes each day, do me a favor—or three, actually. Do one thing that inspires you (even if it's as simple as reading a quote). Do one thing that moves you forward. And acknowledge yourself for one thing you have done so far on this journey. Maybe even dedicate a journal to those three things. I've found that even on days when you feel like you can't go on, when the emotions are too overwhelming and the energy requirements are too great, doing those three things will keep you moving forward.

My wishes for you, friend, are that you are confident in your ability to make decisions based on your truest self rather than what everyone else wants; that you hear the voice of the Spirit clearer than ever before; and that you are forever able to easily access the intuition that God gave you. I hope that you are on track to build a life that you love, with or without your partner, and that you are able to find purpose in life's hard moments.

Be generous with your lives. By opening up to others, you'll prompt people to open up with God.

— MATTHEW 5:15 (MSG)

Ginny Ellsworth grew up in Nashville, Tennessee, raised by a musician-turned-entrepreneur and Broadway-addicted cardiac rehab nurse (who were also devoted parents, by the way). In her early twenties, her pursuit of a journalism degree in Southern California was hijacked by a young marriage and divorce. She landed back in Tennessee and in the fitness industry for several years, training celebrities while scratching the journalism itch by freelancing at small magazines.

After finishing her degree at Tennessee State University, her career volleyed between advertising and storytelling, and her address bounced around the South, mostly in Texas, and later the Emerald Coast of Florida. Her varied experience and passion for the study of human behavior led her to user experience (UX) content design. Still in the booming industry of UX, the forefront of her work always involves asking the right questions and being hyper-aware of human patterns—skills she also applies in her work with coaching and hypnotherapy clients.

Ginny followed the lead of her intuition to study hypnotherapy and cognitive behavioral therapy (CBT). In her intuitive coaching and hypnotherapy practice, she guides clients to shift subconscious thought patterns that keep them stuck, training their subconscious minds to work for them rather than against them in all aspects of life.

She lives at the beach with her pups, travels the word as she pleases, and jets up I-65 to see her nephews in Tennessee as much as she can. She's truly created a life that she loves and is passionate about helping other women do the same.

www.ingramcontent.com/pod-product-compliance
Lightning Source LLC
Chambersburg PA
CBHW051453050726
47593CB00005B/2049